A NEW KIND *of* NORMAL

HOPE-FILLED CHOICES WHEN LIFE TURNS UPSIDE DOWN

CAROL KENT

THOMAS NELSON
Since 1798

NASHVILLE   DALLAS   MEXICO CITY   RIO DE JANEIRO   BEIJING

Published in Nashville, TN, by Thomas Nelson. Thomas Nelson is a trademark of Thomas Nelson, Inc.

Thomas Nelson, Inc. titles may be purchased in bulk for educational, business, fund-raising, or sales promotional use. For information, please e-mail SpecialMarkets@ThomasNelson.com.

All Scripture quotations, unless otherwise marked, are taken from The Holy Bible, New International Version®. Copyright © 1973, 1978, 1984, International Bible Society. Used by permission of Zondervan. All rights reserved.

Other Scripture quotations are taken from the following versions: The Message (MSG) by Eugene H. Peterson. Copyright © 1993, 1994, 1995, 1996, 2000, 2001, 2002. Used by permission of NavPress Publishing Group. All rights reserved. The King James Version of the Bible (KJV). Public domain. The New King James Version® (NKJV®). Copyright © 1982 by Thomas Nelson, Inc. Used by permission. The Holy Bible, New Living Translation® (NLT®). Copyright © 1996. Used by permission of Tyndale House Publishers, Inc., Wheaton, Illinois 60189. All rights reserved. The New American Standard Bible® (NASB®). Copyright © 1960, 1962, 1963, 1968, 1971, 1972, 1973, 1975, 1977, 1995 by The Lockman Foundation. Used by permission. Today's English Version (TEV). Copyright © 1976, second edition copyright © 1992, American Bible Society. The Living Bible (TLB), copyright © 1971 by Tyndale House Publishers, Wheaton, Illinois. Used by permission.

Cover Design: The DesignWorks Group
Interior Design: Casey Hooper

Library of Congress Cataloging-in-Publication Data

Kent, Carol, 1947——
  A new kind of normal : hope-filled choices when life turns upside down / Carol Kent.
    p. cm.
  Includes bibliographical references and index.
  ISBN 10: 0-8499-0199-5 (HC)
  ISBN 13: 978-0-8499-0199-7 (HC)
  ISBN 10: 0-8499-1917-7 (IE)
  ISBN 13: 978-0-8499-1917-6 (IE)
1. Consolation. 2. Suffering–Religious aspects--Christianity. 3. Kent, Carol, 1947- 4. Parent and child--Religious aspects–Christianity. 5. Kent, Jason Paul. 6. Murder--Religious aspects–Christianity. I. Title.
  BV4909.K45 2007
  248.8'6–dc22

                                                                    2006101146

Printed in the United States of America

07 08 09 10 11 RRD 9 8 7 6 5 4 3 2 1

This book is dedicated to people
WHO ARE LIVING IN THEIR OWN
"NEW KIND OF NORMAL."

THEY HAVE ACKNOWLEDGED THAT
UNEXPECTED CIRCUMSTANCES MEAN
LIFE WILL NEVER BE THE SAME AS IT ONCE WAS.

INSTEAD OF RUNNING AWAY OR WITHDRAWING
TO A PRISON OF THEIR OWN MAKING,
THEY CHOOSE TO EMBRACE THE NEW
OPPORTUNITIES AND UNEXPECTED JOYS
THAT CAN ONLY BE KNOWN BY THOSE WHO SAY:

I will survive.
I will persevere.
I will be vulnerable.
I will forgive.
I will trust.
I will hold those I love with open hands.
I will be thankful.
I will choose purposeful action.

I SALUTE YOU!

CONTENTS

CONTENTS

Prologue
FACING SHATTERED DREAMS

$\mathcal{T}$he day was swelteringly hot. Humidity lurked in the house like an unwanted guest that refused to leave. The air-conditioning couldn't keep the temperature down with so many doors open to the outside. Sweat dripped down our faces in dirty little streams as my husband and I directed the movers to place furniture and boxes in the appropriate rooms in the house we had just purchased in Florida.

I found myself speaking out loud to no one in particular: "Anyone who moves to this state has definitely not visited here in the month of July. I have been here less than a day, and I miss the Great Lakes. I miss changing seasons. I miss my friends. I miss my beautiful home along the St. Clair River. I do not want to be here. I hate this weather! I hate this stinking humidity! I hate the reason I had to move here! I want my old life back. I want my peaceful, comfortable, convenient, normal life back!"

"Hey, lady," the mover shouted, "where does this table go?" Wiping away a stray tear, I suddenly realized that the people who were assisting with this move didn't know the difference between a tear and another stream of perspiration. Ah! Something to be thankful for! I didn't want pity. I didn't want compassion. I didn't want to be vulnerable in front of strangers or with anybody else, for that matter, including some relatives who had come to assist with the move. I wanted to be alone in my misery. But that wasn't possible on moving day. So I did what I had done so often before. I sucked in my grief, turned up the "denial" dial on my emotions, wiped my grimy face with a dishtowel, and started directing traffic.

After several interminable hours, the last piece of furniture was off the moving van, and the final box had been piled in the kitchen. What a disgusting mess! *Kind of like my life,* I thought. I was teetering on all-out morbid. Moving across the country was not my idea of fun. I was especially unhappy about being within driving distance of Disney World—that undesirable place where smiling parents brought their perfect families to see Mickey Mouse, Donald Duck, and Snow White. I certainly didn't want to be reminded of fairy tales and happily-ever-after endings.

My life was no longer tidy and unfettered. It was messy, sad, difficult, and unwanted. No one would be selling tickets to advertise my idyllic life. Those days were over. Another chapter of my life had begun, and there was nothing I could do to change it, alter the direction, or manipulate more favorable circumstances. Life as I had known and enjoyed it had turned upside down. My disappointments were gigantic. My hopes were buried in the rubble of recent developments that were so shocking that I was still trying to find any meaning in the fractured pieces of reality that remained.

In one moment in time, everything about the future changed.

❧

If you have read *When I Lay My Isaac Down*, you know about the startling event that shaped my reaction to this move. Gene and I are the parents of an only child—a son named Jason Paul. While still in the womb, we called him Thumper because his activity was constant and his prebirth antics were a precursor of the black belt he earned in karate at the age of eighteen. I was the eldest of six siblings, and as the firstborn grandchild, our son had a personal cheerleading squad surrounding him from earliest days—three sets of grandparents, along with aunts and uncles in abundance. Eighteen first cousins would join us after J.P. was born, and they all adored him. He was as close as a brother to some of them. Our expectations for our son's future were high, and Jason did not disappoint.

He was a witty, high-energy child who endeared himself to anyone who took the time to know him. While in high school, he became president of the National Honor Society and tutored younger students. Jason went on mission trips with his church youth group and volunteered for Habitat for Humanity. Long before graduating in the top twenty in his class, he set his sights on getting into the United States Naval Academy. He received an early invitation to become a cadet at West Point but held out for his heart's desire—becoming a midshipman at the USNA in Annapolis.

The next four years flew by—blood, sweat, tears, exercise, military drills, focus, discipline, more exercise, mental challenges, Commandant Sailing Training Squadron, U.S. Army Airborne Jump School, Midshipmen Leadership Training, U.S. Air Force Combat Survival Training, an Israeli internship program, Search and Rescue Swimmer School, and MINI/BUDS SEAL training on Coronado Island, California. Our son's schedule made my head swim.

Then came the week of graduation in May 1997—complete with color parades, a formal ball, multiple course dinners, and all of the pomp and pageantry a USNA celebration of this magnitude could contain. The fanfare was euphoric. The graduating midshipmen tossed their hats in the air on national television. The diploma was earned, and Jason received a bachelor of science degree in political science while being commissioned as an ensign in the U.S. Navy.

The next year and a half flew by as Jason began nuclear engineering school in Orlando, Florida. Navy Scuba School, U.S. Navy Nuclear Power School, and a lateral transfer to Special Operations—all were accompanied by academic and physical training to become the best defender of freedom the U.S. had in its military human resources arsenal.

There was little time to think of dating. However, J.P.'s involvement in a local church introduced him to the love of his life—and along with this charming woman came two precious and precocious children, aged six and three. Jason and his future wife fell in love over a six-month period of time, and when his orders changed abruptly, sending him to Surface Warfare Officers School in Newport, Rhode Island, they wanted to go together.

We helped plan a wedding that took place in a picturesque suburb of our hometown of Port Huron, Michigan, three weeks later. On the day of our son's marriage celebration in September 1999, Gene and I become grandparents on the same day we became in-laws—and our joy was effusive. The ceremony and reception were followed by a one-night honeymoon before this new family packed up and drove to the East Coast.

Within a short time, there were challenges. The biological father of Jason's stepdaughters was seeking unsupervised visitation, despite allegations of abuse against him that had led the judge during divorce proceedings to require another adult to be present during his visits with his daughters. Jason and his wife sought legal counsel, but they left the attorney's office feeling helpless after being told they might not have enough provable evidence of abuse to keep the court-ordered supervision arrangement intact.

In retrospect, we began to see our son unravel mentally. His fear for the safety of his young stepdaughters consumed his thoughts. Later, our daughter-in-law told us she found him curled up in the embryo position on their bed, pounding his fist into the mattress, repeating, "I don't know how to protect the girls! I don't know how to protect the girls!"

On the morning of October 25, 1999, a phone call shook our life to its foundation. Our son had been arrested for the murder of his wife's first husband—and he was being held in the county jail in Orlando, Florida.

In that one shocking moment, everything changed. That

phone call became a defining moment in time—a marker that has forever divided our past "normal" life from a life we never expected and certainly didn't want. This book is for anyone, like us, who has ever faced an uncertain future because one of those "marker moments" will not let you return to your former definition of "normal."

Mary, the mother of Jesus, faced a defining moment when an angel announced her pregnancy. Little did she know that becoming pregnant before marriage would not be the worst moment of her life. Just over three decades later, the Cross would change everything for Mary. She would discover there was no going back to the former days of nurturing and protecting her young son. He was grown now, and He had to face torture and death *alone*.

For all of us who watch a friend or loved one in the crucible of a life event that, on the surface, is wrecking his life, the agony is palpable. My son is no savior. Mary's son was the Savior of the world. My son is a military-trained young man who believed he was protecting his stepdaughters when he committed his crime. His sentence was not the Cross, but it is life without the possibility of parole.

In a very personal way, I identify with Mary's need to release control of her grown son. I live every day waiting for a miracle of mercy that may never come in this lifetime. The waiting is hard. Painful. Crushing to the spirit. It smashes hope for a better future. It's ugly. Resistant to laughter. Unforgiving. It's an invisible tattoo on my forehead that reads: MOTHER OF A MURDERER. I am living in a new kind of normal.

I invite all of you who are living in circumstances that are different than you expected to read the words of Jerry Sittser. Try to "hear" the voice of a husband and father who received news that his wife, baby daughter, and mother were killed in a car crash by a drunk driver:

> I had no power to control the circumstances that altered the course of our lives . . . But I discovered soon after the accident that I still had power to determine the course my life would take, however limited that power seemed at the time. I had the power to choose how I would respond and whether or not I would trust in God.[1]

This book is about choices—not the kind we place on goal charts, but the choices we all need to make when our carefully developed life plan takes a U-turn or comes to a sudden halt. It's about discovering fresh hope and renewed courage when we would rather give up. It's about willfully choosing to make the future better, even if we don't receive a tangible benefit for making the effort. It's about choosing not to waste the sorrow. It's about giving hope to others in the middle of our brokenness and tears, because it is all we have to offer. And because it is all we have to give, it is enough.

I think Tim Hansel says it best. Following a mountain-climbing accident that resulted in continuing physical challenges, he wrote, "I had a choice. I knew by now that the damage was permanent, and that pain would be a companion for the rest of my journey. I had to learn a whole new way of living or fold up my cards. The deck was stacked. The life I'd always known was never to be again."[2]

Perhaps you're feeling like folding up your cards. Making hope-filled choices may be the furthest thing from your mind right now. But I challenge you, as I have been challenged, to consider your life from some different angles. Are you willing to take the chance that your "new normal" might offer benefits you never expected? Perhaps even joy? I realize that may sound like a big stretch—but, really, what do you have to lose?

I don't promise easy answers. In fact, you might wind up with more questions than before you began this journey to a new normal. There will be frustration, hurt, and more bumps in the road. But your movement can be purposeful—in the direction of hope.

Take the risk. Join hands with me on this journey. It is all we have. And it is enough.

one
SYMPATHY CARDS AND RAZOR WIRE

When Despair Tries to Take Me Under . . .
I CHOOSE LIFE

> LIFE ISN'T LIKE A BOOK.
> LIFE ISN'T LOGICAL OR SENSIBLE OR ORDERLY.
> LIFE IS A MESS MOST OF THE TIME.
> AND THEOLOGY MUST BE LIVED
> IN THE MIDST OF THAT MESS.
> —CHARLES COLSON

It was Christmas morning, and my husband, Gene, and I were standing in line at the prison, waiting to get through the razor wire so we could visit our son. The stark buildings were not decorated with colored lights, evergreen wreaths, and holiday bows. There were no Christmas carols amplified over loudspeakers, and there was nothing celebratory in sight that would remind a passerby that December 25 was the most notable holiday of the year.

Actually, even the idea of a "passerby" was remote. To find Hardee Correctional Institution on deserted State Road 62, we routinely scanned the landscape from the highway and looked for the prison water tower. Once it was identified, we knew we were getting closer as the image grew larger against the rough and undeveloped landscape on this little-traveled road. The driveway from the road to the prison was a quarter mile long, ending with the cement lot where visitors parked while they spent time with their family members inside this maximum-security facility.

How different this Christmas was from my growing-up years! It was also considerably unlike the last holiday season Jason spent at home. My mind flashed back to December 1999. Jason had married just three months earlier, and he brought his family to our home in Michigan for what was sure to be a joy-filled holiday. We were eager to make lasting memories with our new stepgranddaughters.

The girls burst into the house with eager enthusiasm and rushed to the Christmas tree. "Wow!" our six-year-old said. "It's so beautiful!" The three-year-old was already chasing the cat, hoping for a little nose-to-nose intimacy with our furry Himalayan feline. I saw both girls scanning the brightly wrapped gifts that had been placed with love under the Christmas tree.

"Some of those gifts are for you, girls. We're so glad you are here!"

Their faces beamed, and I could see them evaluating whether they knew us well enough to risk an abrupt move. Gene and I must have given the right signal, because they dove into the pile of gifts, checking to see which packages had their names on them. The love I felt for these gorgeous little girls and the delight we experienced in having Jason and his new family join us for the holidays is beyond words.

That Christmas is like a treasured mosaic of giggling children, turkey and mashed potatoes, strawberry ice cream Jell-O, and homemade, decorated cookies—lots of cookies and hot chocolate (with marshmallows, of course). Our son and his wife were in the throes of young love, and I enjoyed watching them hold each other by the fireplace. Their love was deep and wide and tender and compassionate. I found myself wiping tears of joy, knowing my son had met a woman who was ideal for him. On Christmas Eve other relatives joined us, and the little girls were loved by all as their high energy ignited the house with the extravagant hope that should belong to every child.

None of us knew it would be our last Christmas to celebrate with such reckless abandon and with an unencumbered sense of "normal." Never again would our family conform to a standard holiday experience or to the type of Christmas celebration we thought we would enjoy for the rest of our lives. Jason's incarceration changed that picture forever.

I suddenly lurched back into the reality of where I stood in the prison visitation line, now six Christmases later. Three women were ahead of us in the line, and their conversation was loud enough that I could easily overhear what they were saying. They, too, were relatives of inmates—and I had instant respect for these women who chose to come to the prison visitation yard on a day that is normally spent on feasting, merriment, and gift giving in the comfortable surroundings of home, family, and friends. However, I wasn't prepared for the wave of emotion that engulfed me as I heard their banter:

"This is my last Christmas to stand in this line. My son is getting out in eight months."

"Oh," another mother said wistfully, "we have eight more years before we'll be spending Christmas Day at home with our son, but we're going to make it."

Another voice chimed in: "My husband will be home for Christmas in four more years. The kids and I can't wait."

Despite bursting into completely unexpected tears, I managed to smile at the three women in front of me. We were strangers in a social club we never expected to join—women from completely different backgrounds with a shared bond: a family member who was incarcerated.

"I'm so happy for all of you," I blurted out in a gesture of forced enthusiasm. But the tears rolling down my cheeks told the truth. My heart was broken, and I could no longer pretend that everything was going to be fine. My son was *never* coming home for Christmas dinner. He would be behind razor wire for the rest of his life—and today he was only thirty-one years old.

Inside, my heart felt pangs of anger and jealousy. All of the joy-filled comments I heard from the women moments earlier were drowned out by an ugly voice inside me that taunted, *Your son will never walk in freedom again. All of the rest of the Christmases of your life will be spent standing in the visitation line at the prison. You'll be patted down as you go through while a stranger looks into your mouth to see if you are hiding an illegal substance and runs hands around your bra, looking for contraband. You will be scrutinized as if you are a criminal every time you visit your son for the rest of your life. You are a loser.*

One thing was crystal clear. I had "a new kind of normal" that had nothing to do with the life I envisioned for myself, my only child, my family, and my ministry. The son of my womb, the boy-turned-man I loved so much, was not coming home—*ever*. I was running out of hope—hope that any of the appeals would result in a favorable court ruling, hope that our son would ever walk in freedom again, hope that we would ever be together in our home on a Christmas morning, hope for the happiness that everyone else appeared to have. I felt all alone in my despair.

BRIGHT BEGINNINGS

Jason Paul Kent was born on a crisp fall day on a picture-perfect Sunday morning. To make the story even more idyllic, we were living in Fremont, Michigan, the town that was built on the success of the Gerber Baby Foods Corporation, and we were in the hospital "built by Gerber." Jason weighed in at 5 pounds, 14 ounces, and he measured 17 inches in length. A tiny bundle to be sure, but a genuine Gerber baby. After nine hours of painful labor, our long-awaited firstborn child, a son, was placed in my arms. Had I known ahead of time how painful childbirth is, I would have pleaded for drugs (or at least requested an epidural), but I was a mind-over-matter kind of woman and never asked for help if I could muscle through the pain. Our baby boy was worth it!

To make the day even more spectacular, my next-door neighbor, Mary, gave birth to a baby girl on the very same day in the same hospital. What a celebration! Family members and friends joined us in spreading the good news. "Gene and Carol have a boy!" This birth took place five years after our wedding day, and the grandparents had been waiting a long time for their first grandchild. To say that Jason was instantly enveloped with love is the understatement of the century.

The gift of life—a tiny infant wrapped in a flannel blanket, with ten tiny toes and ten delicate fingers, a wobbly head attached to a scrawny, exquisitely gorgeous pink body. A cute button nose and cherry-colored cheeks. That small bundle held all of the promise Gene and I needed for the assurance of a bright, purposeful, and joy-filled future. With God's help, we were determined to be great parents.

As Jason grew older, we got him a "big-boy" bed. It didn't take him long to realize that Gene and I would stay at his side longer at bedtime and stroke his head and hair if he kept talking. There were many conversations and prayers, along with questions and answers during our tucking-in ritual.

I often reminded him, "J.P, always remember God has something very special for you to do with your life. You can be anything He wants you to be. I can hardly wait to see what God has planned for you. I've been praying for you since before you were born."

One of Gene's early activities with our son was to read aloud to him. As soon as Jason was capable of listening to an entire chapter of a book, Gene decided to introduce him to C. S. Lewis. Over a period of several months, Gene read all seven books in The Chronicles of Narnia to a very animated and energetic listener. I once caught Jason searching for Narnia in the back of an antique wardrobe closet. If the mind could conceive it, he could believe it. He was ready to join Peter, Susan, Edmund, and Lucy in the land of Turkish Delight. "Adventure" could have been Jason's middle name.

As Jason entered his teens, "my guys" loved running together—and they would often challenge each other with physical exercise goals. When Jason was in his senior year at the U.S. Naval Academy, Gene and Jason trained for and ran a half-marathon together. They challenged each other to physical and intellectual excellence. I loved listening and joining in as they bantered back and forth about global events, politics, and controversial issues. No matter what the topic, they would find a place for humor—both appropriate and irreverent. I would shake my head in mock disapproval, but my mother heart held those moments with tender gratitude to God for giving our family such a close and caring relationship. There were occasional conflicts, especially over teenage bedroom décor, but they were short-lived. Gene and I quickly decided to only make a big deal over things that were immoral or illegal. Most other issues were not worth a major conflict.

Between Jason's sophomore and junior years of high school, we heard about an academic Christian camp in Manitou Springs, Colorado, called Summit Ministries. They combined an aggressive academic program in Christian worldview studies with a rigorous athletic program. It sounded like a custom fit for Jason's growing desire to make a difference with his life. He couldn't wait to go, and during the two weeks he was there, he had a "defining moment."

One evening soon after his return, I found him journaling in his room. His Bible was open, and he was deep in study. As Gene and I talked more with Jason about his time at Summit, he said, "Mom and Dad, I really believe God wants me to serve in military, or maybe even in political leadership, and I believe the best place I could get prepared to do that would be at the U.S. Naval Academy."

FROM ANNAPOLIS TO ORLANDO

The rest of the story is history. Jason's nomination came from Congressman David Bonior, followed by an appointment from the Academy. On a hot day in late June 1993 we packed up the car to drive Jason to the next season of his life—"plebe summer" in Annapolis. With more than a few nostalgic tears, I marveled at how fast his high school years had gone by, while simultaneously anticipating his future that was sure to be filled with international travel and a wide range of opportunities to use his mind, his faith, and his determined focus to make a positive difference in this world.

Four years later, the whole family gathered in Annapolis for graduation week, and only two years after that, our son was married and enjoying being a father to two beautiful girls. Whenever our granddaughters visited us, they hunted for dress-up clothes. My closet was ransacked as they turned "flowy" skirts and silk scarves into ballroom attire. They found my high heels and jewelry and transformed themselves into regal princesses. The music was turned up, and our dancing girls tirelessly entertained us for hours on end. I had no idea being "Grammy" could be so much fun!

Gene would take the girls out for breakfast and call it "having a date with Grampy." As soon as they were invited out, they would rush to dress up in their favorite attire so they would look smashingly gorgeous at Perkins Restaurant or Bob Evans. Those eateries had never known such glamour—and Gene was in his glory!

I think God, in His mercy, doesn't let us see the future because we wouldn't be able to enjoy the present.

THE PHONE CALL

We were looking forward to watching this young family of four thrive—but everything changed on a Sunday afternoon in the parking lot of a Sweet Tomatoes Restaurant in Orlando, Florida. We didn't get the news until 12:35 the next morning when the familiar ring of the phone pierced the darkness and startled us from peaceful sleep.

Gene picked up the receiver, and the newspapers, television reports, and court records bear witness to the defining moment we were about to experience—one so very different from our son's just seven years earlier at summer camp. This moment turned out to be the pivotal one between our "old normal" and the life that would never be the same again.

Jason had been arrested for the murder of his wife's first husband, Douglas Miller Jr. I was immediately overcome by nausea. Disbelief. Sobbing. Heart palpitations. Sick waves of reality mixed with despair. A nightmare of gigantic proportion. Impossible facts—that Jason shot the gun, four bullets in the back of the victim. A stray bullet hit a van with children inside. No one was hurt, but the possibility was devastating. Not our boy! "No-o-o-o-o! Please, God, let this be a horrible dream!" I felt as if I'd been kicked in the gut by a horse. I could not walk. Doubled over on all fours, I crawled to the bathroom to vomit.

The events that followed were surreal. Jason's mug shot on the front page of the *Orlando Sentinel*. Attorneys. The prosecutor.

Necessary legal procedures. Then deep waves of sadness for the father, stepmother, and sister of the deceased. While we prepared for a trial for first-degree murder, their family was planning a funeral. Our thoughts were a jumbled mess.

How did this happen?

Where did we go wrong?

What distorted our son's sense of righteousness in such a bizarre and unthinkable way?

Where was God? Why did He let this happen?

I'm going to be sick again.

WANTING TO DIE

Gene and I stumbled through the next forty-eight hours in much the same way other people live one second at a time when their lives fall apart without warning. I literally gasped for air as I thought of my son in a maximum-security jail surrounded by rapists and thugs. The thought was more than my heart could bear. In between my sobs, I tried to help Gene make a long list of people who needed to be contacted.

Almost ritualistically, I went through the house, closing the blinds. I didn't want reporters at my door. I didn't want sunshine falling on my tears. I wanted to curl up and die. Breathing came with difficulty. Moaning cries choked words. I wondered if anyone had ever actually died of a broken heart.

Gene left for Florida to move our daughter-in-law and the girls from Panama City, where Jason had been in dive school with the navy, to Orlando, where he was now incarcerated. Soon after, a call came from Jason. I accepted the charges for the telephone call from the 33rd Street jail and listened while my son told me he had just been beaten by ten inmates who jumped him when he walked into his cell.

I could hardly breathe as I heard him describe the beating—in the eyes, constant kicking in the face, both of his front teeth broken. As he told me the details of the attack, he was choking back sobs. Then as suddenly as it began, the call ended with an automatic cutoff through the phone system at the jail. I later found out the beating happened while corrections officers looked on, apparently enjoying the entertainment.

I was alone in the house when the call ended. I raised my hands toward heaven and could identify with Jesus as He said, "My God, my God, why have you forsaken me?" (Mark 15:34). I flashed back to hearing a pastor say that those words, uttered by Christ on the cross, really meant, "My God, my God, why are you so far from the words of my guttural groaning?" I now under-stood what Jesus meant. *Guttural groaning* was the only way to describe the sound coming out of me. I wanted to die. Quit. Leave the agony behind and skip the rest of life.

And then the "mama" part of me kicked in. I realized our son needed his parents more than he had ever needed us. The next day, I left for Florida to see Jason. As he rounded the corner and faced me behind a Plexiglas window in the visitation area, he was in wrist and ankle shackles, connected by chains to each limb, and he was fresh from the beating that could have taken his life. As our eyes met, I noticed the jagged front teeth of my broken and bruised son.

Through fresh tears of my own, the words tumbled out. "Jason Paul Kent, nothing you could ever do would stop my unconditional love for you, Son." That meeting was mostly about tears. Being there for each other. Knowing we couldn't fix what had already happened. Realizing that nothing about the future would be normal. The fifteen-minute visit ended far too soon. I walked to the parking lot and sat in my car for a long time, weeping, unable to see enough through the torrent of tears to drive away. A piece of my heart stayed at the jail—a part I felt was vital for my heart to continue beating at all.

Nothing about this emerging journey was familiar, comfortable, or desired. It was like a trip to another country—to a foreign land where our family didn't belong. I wanted to return to my old normal. But there was no going back.

ANOTHER MOTHER'S STORY

Mary, the mother of Jesus, certainly knew what it was like to see her son in a worst-case scenario. Her son was the Messiah, the promised Savior of the world. One day, many people were crowding the streets of Jerusalem for Passover. There was an ominous tension in the air. Mary probably stayed close to the Galilean women.

On Friday, as they gathered in the temple area, the women noticed a crowd of people heading toward Golgotha, on the edge of town. Someone in the group must have yelled, "What's going on?"

Another responded, "They say Jesus is being crucified. Let's follow the crowd and find out what's happening."

My son can never be compared to the Son of God, but I can identify with the panicked thoughts that must have been in Mary's heart at that moment. She was a mother in pain.

But He's my son. No! No! No! Surely you can see His pure motives.
This is happening too fast. You don't understand why He did what He did.
Please let me get through to Him. I must be near my boy. He needs His
mother. I want Him to see my love. It will give Him strength.

By the time Mary saw her son, it was obvious Jesus had been severely beaten. They called it a scourging. According to historical facts, the whip used for such torture was constructed of nine strips of leather with bits of bone, metal, or glass attached to the ends. When the beating was done, often the straps would reach all the way around from the back to the abdomen, tearing away the flesh and creating deep wounds. No wonder Isaiah the prophet said that "his appearance was so disfigured beyond that of any man and his form marred beyond human likeness" (Isa. 52:14).

At the crucifixion scene, Mary viewed the unthinkable. Her son's broken body was nailed to a tree. She saw Jesus endure raw, torturous agony, while people stood by and ridiculed Him. The combination of seeing His physical pain and hearing the taunts from the crowd as they reviled her now thirty-three-year-old son must have crushed her spirit.

The Bible tells us that Mary stood by the cross. "Near the cross of Jesus stood his mother, his mother's sister, Mary the wife of Clopas, and Mary Magdalene. When Jesus saw his mother there, and the disciple whom he loved standing nearby, he said to his mother, 'Dear woman, here is your son,' and to the disciple, 'Here is your mother.' From that time on, this disciple took her into his home" (John 19:25–27).

For Mary, choosing life at that moment meant going to live with John, because she would never again have her son to live with. In the culture of that day, a widow normally would have been cared for by one of her children (perhaps one of the brothers of Jesus mentioned in Mark 3:31). It is significant that Jesus, the oldest son, asked the loyal friend who stayed with Him during His final hours, John, to provide comfort and provision for His mother. (Some Bible commentators suggest that Salome, the wife of Zebedee and the mother of James and John, was Mary's sister. If this was the case, then John would have been Mary's nephew.)

Following her son's wishes by going to live in John's household was not Mary's first challenging choice in life, but it may have been her most difficult. Perhaps she felt like dying alongside her son, but she chose to go on without Him. She was no doubt beyond bereft, even if she had a clue about God's bigger plan. One thing is certain—she didn't curl up in the fetal position and give herself over to despair. When all the disciples except John gave up all hope and abandoned Jesus, Mary, His mother, stood as close to Him as she could get until He took His last breath.

IDENTIFYING WITH MARY

My son was not dying—but after two and a half years and seven postponements of his trial, he was convicted of first-degree murder and sentenced to life in prison without the possibility of parole—ever! That is my new normal. Gene and I have to decide every day that we will choose life in the middle of devastating circumstances instead of giving in to emotional death, depression, discouragement, and defeat.

There are many kinds of crucibles in life that forever alter the future some of us thought would be ours:

- A child born with a disability
- Loss of a job or ministry position
- A son or daughter's addiction to drugs and/or alcohol
- The premature death of a loved one
- Financial devastation
- A tragic accident that brings pain and disability
- A spouse who leaves for someone else
- A friend who betrays us
- Loss of control due to aging and/or physical challenges
- Relentless emotional or physical pain
- Infertility
- Self-loathing due to the wrong choices of the past
- Desire for marriage, with no candidate in sight
- Sexual assault on ourselves or someone we love
- Spiritual disillusionment due to grave loss
- Victimization due to a violent crime
- The arrest of a spouse or child

The list is endless. All of us need to fill in the blank for ourselves. But most of us can identify with what it feels like to give up what we treasure most to the God who loves us more than we love our child, spouse, positions, security, reputations, and dreams for the future. If you have ever wanted to "check out" instead of choosing life, you might identify with author and speaker Louise Tucker Jones as she describes her "new kind of normal."

I WILL SURVIVE!

It was a year of extremes. My husband and I celebrated our twenty-fifth wedding anniversary. Our prodigal daughter came home for Christmas with a newborn baby. Our oldest son graduated from college. And our youngest son's cardiologist deemed him at great risk for a stroke, a fatal cardiac arrhythmia, and congestive heart failure.

My emotions were spent, my body exhausted, and my mind overwhelmed, but I trudged on. That's what I always did. I had been walking this tightrope of fear for our medically fragile and developmentally disabled son his whole life. Jay was born with Down syndrome and at six weeks old was diagnosed with congenital heart disease. At fourteen months, a heart catheterization revealed the severity and the devastating report that our child's condition could not be corrected. We were given little hope that Jay would live into adolescence. Not only did Jay defy those odds, but he lived life fully and intentionally, enjoying our vacations at the beach alongside his brother and sister. Now, here he was, fifteen years old and doing well, in spite of the heart disease.

Then it happened. One day while Jay was standing at the sink, helping me wash and dry dishes, he suddenly looked at me, turned deathly pale, and fell into my arms, unconscious. No warning. The doctor had told us that a fatal cardiac arrhythmia would leave no time for doctors or an ambulance. It would be sudden death.

My heart was racing, the blood pounding in my temples, as I screamed, "God, please don't let my son die! Please don't let him die!" I lowered Jay's body to the floor and grabbed the phone, punching in 911. My words came so quickly they sounded as one. "My-son-has-severe-heart-disease-and-has-just-passed-out!" I yelled into the phone. I was more than scared. I was terrified.

The paramedics arrived within minutes. Jay had regained consciousness, and we were racing to the hospital in an ambulance. My prayers continued silently. *God, please don't let Jay die. Please don't let him die!* I knew nothing else to pray.

A couple of hours later, the crisis had passed, and I took my son home. He had fainted because of mild dehydration due to a virus. His heart had nothing to do with it.

At home, I locked myself in my bedroom, fell on my knees, and sobbed, thanking God for sparing my son. But deep in my heart I knew there would eventually be another crisis, another emergency call, and the next one might not end favorably. I wondered how I could survive if something happened to Jay. He was my "constant" in life.

In the years after Jay was diagnosed, my "new normal" with a developmentally disabled child became my "normal normal." Staying home with him day after day. Always on alert for signs of infection. Guarding Jay from every possible illness. Translating his needs to doctors and professionals when they couldn't understand his speech. I was the friend he didn't have, playing games and watching TV with him. I was his homeschool teacher as well as Sunday school teacher. This was my life, and even though it was sometimes difficult, it was my normal.

But something happened that day when I saw Jay's limp body lying on the floor. Remembering the cardiologist's predictions, I kept thinking, *One day this will be for real. One day he won't wake up.* The thought of losing my son *for real* threw me into a downward spiral. Each time I tried to stop my negative thoughts, they barreled into my mind with greater force. *I have to find a way to preserve Jay's life,* I ruminated. *I have to be perfect in my decisions concerning him. There is no room for mistakes.* Obsessive fear often held me in a vise grip.

Day after day, week after week, the fear continued. I was sliding into a pit of despair and didn't know what was happening to me. I shook inside but didn't know why. I hardly slept at night, and when I did, I usually woke up screaming from night terrors. I was also dealing with the symptoms of perimenopause. The mood swings and hot flashes made it harder for me to cope with other difficult family dynamics. Our oldest son, Aaron, had moved ten hours away from home, and our daughter, now married, was living in an abusive relationship. I feared for her and the baby. My husband and I did not have good communication at the time, so I felt totally isolated. I wondered who I could talk to. How could I explain what was happening to me? Who would understand what I was going through? It felt as if my body was shutting down. My fatigue was so great I could hardly get out of bed in the morning. When I finally managed to get myself up, I would go to the kitchen and grab some protein to try to calm the constant shaking, both inside and outside my body. I knew something inside me was broken, but I had no idea how to fix it or where to find help.

Finally, one morning I simply could not get out of bed. My husband took me to a multitude of doctors who diagnosed me with clinical depression, a chemical imbalance, hormonal imbalance, sleep deprivation, and a panic disorder. My panic was so great I couldn't even answer the phone, much less take care of myself or my son. All I could do was sit on the bed, wrap my arms around myself in a tight hug, and rock and cry.

For a full month, someone stayed with me around the clock. My husband, Carl, took vacation time from work in order to care for Jay and me; then Carl's aunt came from out of town and spent two weeks, allowing him to return to work. She adored Jay, and I felt safe with her. After she left, a few women from my church took turns coming to my home to help me when needed. They set up a schedule so that one of them was always available to come if necessary. I just had to call.

However, the darkness was so thick, no one could penetrate it. I felt I was in a deep pit with no way out. And though I took medication, I felt no hope that I'd get well. Depression strips away all optimism and steals your dreams and joy. I was even afraid of the medication, but I took it. I also visited a psychologist twice a week for counseling, where I talked about my life—what it was like before depression and what it was like now. The therapist validated my feelings and encouraged me, but wellness was slow in coming.

On the advice of the doctor, my husband went with me to many of the counseling sessions. It was important that he learn what clinical depression was and how he could help me. It also helped us communicate better. Clinical depression is more than being a little sad or unhappy. It's not about having a bad day or a rough week. Depression is void of emotion and human connection. It's a place where *living* is harder than *dying*. For the first time, I understood why some people take their own lives. I had always considered suicide the most selfish act a person could do, but now I had a different perspective. At one point, I took my husband's gun from the top shelf of his closet and held it in my hand, marveling at how easy it would be to end my life—to escape this horrendous despair. But the thought of what this would do to my husband and children stopped me. I put away the gun and prayed more fervently than ever for God to heal me. I knew instinctively that God's hand was the only one strong enough to pull me out of my darkness.

During this time I pulled away from everything social, including church. My panic was just too great. But as I pulled away from others, I cuddled closer to God. Even though I often felt unlovable and hopeless, I knew in my mind that God loved me. I apologized to God over and over, feeling certain I was a great disappointment to Him, but I never stopped praying. Every day I cried, prayed, and read Scripture. I prayed for God to help my family cope. But most of all, I prayed for Him to stay with me, to walk though this valley with me, and to reveal Himself to me in a brand-new way. Every night I dreaded closing my eyes because of the nightmares.

Several godly women came into my life during this time and helped me physically, mentally, emotionally, and spiritually. A wonderful friend from Houston had also experienced the ravages of depression and wrote me encouraging notes or called to tell me that God loved me and I was going to get well. The wife of a retired minister in my church "adopted" me and came to my home to teach me needlepoint, often bringing a meal with her. Another friend offered to stay with Jay when Carl took me to my doctor or counseling appointments.

One friend encouraged me to keep the Word of God in my sight and in my mind at all times, so I searched the Bible for verses on fear, such as, "God has not given us the spirit of fear but of power and of love and of a sound mind" (2 Tim. 1:7 NKJV) and "Fear not, for I am with you; be not dismayed, for I am your God. I will strengthen you, yes, I will help you, I will uphold you with My righteous right hand" (Isa. 41:10 NKJV). I tried to memorize them, but I also copied the verses on index cards and taped them to my kitchen cabinets and bathroom mirror so I could recite a promise from God when panic hit and my mind refused to recall any truth from memory. I listened to Christian radio programs and made needlepoint pieces with the name of Jesus on them, just wanting to keep His name in front of me and my hands busy. I played Scripture tapes at night as I went to sleep in an attempt to counter the horrendous nightmares.

Gradually, I learned to center my thoughts on the Lord and depend on Him in a way I had never done. I still had so little strength and energy I could not depend on myself. My husband and my friends helped in all the tangible ways necessary, but only God could change my thinking—renew my mind and bring me hope. In the midst of this darkness, I eventually found a God I had never known. He walked with me through the Slough of Despond. He didn't miraculously remove me from it, but He waded through the muck right beside me. Just Him and me. He never left me alone, and I loved Him as I had never loved Him before.

It was months before I was able to attend a church service. Though I watched programs on TV every Sunday, I longed for my own church family. I especially missed the music, even though I often played worship tapes at home. Finally, one Wednesday evening, I drove myself to the church, a huge feat in itself. I waited until the congregation left. I still could not deal with people socially without severe panic. When the crowd diminished, I walked into the sanctuary and sat on the back row and listened to the choir practice for the Sunday service. I so desperately needed to hear the praises to God. The music was like water for a thirsty traveler. I just sat and absorbed the vocal harmonies, the words, and the atmosphere.

Weeks passed before I finally attended a Sunday worship service. I was fearful of having a panic attack yet excited about going. I now had such an awe of God's presence that I could hardly wait to worship in His house. I felt elated just walking into the church. My heart was ready for worship. Friends told me I looked great, but everything felt so different. The social atmosphere in which I found myself felt unnatural, even disturbing. People were talking and laughing, even after the service began. A couple of women in front of me talked nonstop through the first song, and I wanted to scream, "Don't you realize this is a holy place?" My time alone with God had been so deep, so personal, so profound that I was unprepared for the church atmosphere.

Like Moses, God had called me to a sacred place. My sandals had long been removed as I stood on holy ground with my Lord. I would never lose those moments, but I had to come down from the mountain. It was time to live again. Time to be a wife and mother again. To drive my car, shop for groceries, and even help others. Again, I had to take responsibility for Jay's health and his needs. To make decisions. To become independent again. I had to find a "new normal."

It was a full year before I truly felt whole again. Even after that, I visited my psychologist monthly and continued taking medication for the panic disorder, which never totally went away. I wish I could say that today all my fears are gone, that it is easy to have faith and trust God each day, no matter what happens. The truth is I struggle like everyone else. But one thing I have learned. Though I may sometimes question God's ways, I never question His love. He proved His love for me in the pit.

Fifteen years have passed, and Jay is now thirty years old. He still lives at home, where he and I spend our days together, since he is unable to work outside the home due to his compromised immune system. I try to make each day an adventure, even if it is just playing a game of Bingo, watching a video, or taking Jay on his daily trip to Sonic for a Coke. Jay loves church and seldom misses a Sunday, always wearing a snazzy tie from his collection of two hundred neckties. Jay and his dad are very close as well. Carl takes over much of our son's care when he gets home from work, which allows me time to myself and with friends. And though Carl and I call Jay our miracle, there have been more scary moments along the way. More trips to the hospital in speeding ambulances and always more prayers for healing.

The chemical imbalance in my brain requires me to stay on a low dose of medication. Though I would prefer to be medication free, I am thankful for meds that allow me to lead what I now call a "normal" life. And though I realize I may still have to walk through the fire in the future, my Bible tells me I will not be consumed (Isa. 43:2). It also tells me that I am precious and honored in God's sight and that He loves me with an everlasting love (Isa. 43:4; Jer. 31:3). That's hope-filled news, no matter what kind of "normal" we experience in this life.[1]

CHOOSING LIFE WITH OPEN HANDS

Soon after our son's arrest for murder was front-page news, we received many comforting cards in our mailbox. The cards kept coming over a period of several months, and we collected them in a large basket.

One day while I was alone in the house, depression was pulling me into the grip of despair. I picked up the basket to go through the notes people had sent us. I felt a sense of shock and sadness when I realized how many *sympathy* cards we had received—the kind people send when someone has died and the family is planning a funeral. I screamed at the top of my lungs, "My son is *alive*! He is not dead. He is *alive*!"

The heart-wrenching truth was that someone else's son was dead at the hands of my son.

We faced the most important decision in this hellish journey. Would we die too—emotionally, spiritually, and even physically—or would we choose life? We eventually came to a place of realizing we could not change the facts of what had happened, but we could decide how we would live our lives in the middle of razor wire, sympathy cards, and deep disappointment. Choosing life, instead of a slow death, has been the beginning of rediscovering hope.

Ken Gire says, "When suffering shatters the carefully kept vase that is our lives, God stoops to pick up the pieces. But he doesn't put them back together as a restoration project patterned after our former selves. Instead, he sifts through the rubble and selects some of the shards as raw material for another project—a mosaic that tells the story of redemption."[2]

Jesus Himself said, "I came so they can have real and eternal life, more and better life than they ever dreamed of" (John 10:10 MSG). Life instead of death. Hope instead of despair. Even joy in the midst of terrible sorrow. A new kind of living—harder, but better in some ways, than before. Maddening because we hate the process but richer because of the pain.

Life. Pure and simple. It's a choice. It's a new kind of normal.

GOD'S POWER IN YOUR NEW KIND OF NORMAL

At some point, most of us will encounter a challenging situation that permanently alters the rest of our lives. For you, it probably won't be having a child arrested for murder, but it might be a knock at the door, a middle-of-the-night phone call, or a diagnosis from the doctor that changes the future as you envisioned it. It could be that your married child gets a divorce and you will no longer have opportunities to spend time with your grandchildren because they will have moved away with the other spouse. It may be that all of your friends are having babies and you've been told you will never be able to carry a child.

You may not spend your future Christmases the way I spent my last Christmas, but special holidays will nonetheless be different than you anticipated. What you once thought of as "normal" will be adjusted to a "new kind of normal." The question is, how will you respond to your new normal? Will you withdraw from society and close the blinds on communication with other people, focusing only on your personal pain and deep grief, or will you choose to live a meaningful and vibrant life, even if it's different from the life you always wanted? Will you make choices based on unshakable truth that will not only enhance the quality of your own life but also bring renewed hope and fresh courage to people in your sphere of influence?

1. How do you define the word *normal?* Are you someone who appreciates a predictable pattern in life, or do you adjust well to sudden change, good or bad?

2. Looking back on your life, what was a "normal" Christmas like for you? Do you have happy memories of that holiday, or was it often a challenging season?

3. Briefly describe a time when an unexpected crisis meant your life was not going to turn out as planned. What were your feelings at the time? Did you deal with the situation in a constructive or destructive way? Be specific.

4. Think about your view of Scripture. Have you encountered a time when it's been challenging to believe Jesus came to bring us abundant life? Jesus proclaimed, "I am come that they might have life, and that they might have it more abundantly" (John 10:10 KJV). What does "abundant life" look like when you are living in a new kind of normal? Does this Scripture encourage you, or does it frustrate you?

5. Mary, the mother of Jesus, faced what some might say is the ultimate pain for a mother to endure—watching her son die an excruciating death by crucifixion. Which is harder for you: to suffer yourself or to accept that people you love are suffering? On a scale of 1 to 10 (with 10 being highest), how do you rate your ability to encourage others

to hold on to hope when their lives have taken a downward turn? Identify one person whom you will intentionally encourage to hold on to hope this week. Write down what you will do to provide tangible help for someone who is living in a new kind of normal.

6. Think about Ken Gire's statement: "When suffering shatters the carefully kept vase that is our lives, God stoops to pick up the pieces. But he doesn't put them back together as a restoration project patterned after our former selves. Instead, he sifts through the rubble and selects some of the shards as raw material for another project—a mosaic that tells the story of redemption."[3] It usually takes a long time to find meaning and purpose when you are living in the middle of devastating circumstances. If you are up to writing the story of how God is helping you to find "redemption" in the midst of an experience that has altered or outright shattered your dreams, journal about how He used the "shards" in your experience as the raw material for a renewed ability to choose life—perhaps not the life you expected but the "redemptive life" you now have. If it's too early in your journey to chronicle what happened, that's okay. For now, decide to move in the direction of life instead of slipping into self-pity, debilitating doubt, and the stranglehold of fear. Choosing life is the first step in getting a foothold in your own new kind of normal.

two

THE BATTLE OF THE MIND AND HEART

When I Wonder What God Could Possibly Be Thinking . . . I CHOOSE TRUST

RUTHLESS TRUST ULTIMATELY COMES DOWN TO THIS:
FAITH IN THE PERSON OF JESUS
AND HOPE IN HIS PROMISE.
IN SPITE OF ALL DISCONCERTING APPEARANCES,
WE STARE DOWN DEATH WITHOUT NERVOUSNESS
AND ANTICIPATE RESURRECTION
SOLELY BECAUSE JESUS HAS SAID,
"YOU HAVE MY WORD ON IT."
—BRENNAN MANNING

The cell phone rang during a midday break at a women's conference in St. Louis. It was our daughter-in-law.

"Mom and Dad, I think I'm having a miscarriage." Her voice was shaking. "I'm spotting, and I don't know what to do. I'm so afraid."

Only a week earlier, Jason had told us the grand news that

they were expecting, and we were thrilled for them and for us. A baby—our *grandbaby!*—would be joining our family.

Our daughter-in-law continued. "Jason is away diving all weekend, and I don't have any way to reach him." At that time our son was in the most intensive dive school the navy offers—on mixed gases at low ocean depths. It was one of those rare seasons in life when what he *loved* to do—dive—matched what he was *paid* to do by the U.S. government.

An examination at the hospital in Panama City confirmed that our daughter-in-law had miscarried. It was a very sad day. Jason and his wife lost their much-wanted baby. It was their second miscarriage. We lost our next grandchild. But no one could reach Jason.

We flew home on Sunday, and early the following Monday morning, the middle-of-the-night call came from our son's wife, announcing the shocking news of Jason's arrest for murder. We were so stunned that we hardly had a moment to grieve the loss of the baby before plunging into the legal details of our son's case. As the reality of these huge challenges confronted us, I felt like screaming. What poured out of me on that day after my son's arrest for murder was part prayer, part anger, part honesty, and part exaggeration, but deep authenticity:

> *Hello, God! I am hurting too badly to put a fist in Your face—but at this moment our loss and our grief are so intense I really wonder if I can trust You. Where were You when J.P. and his wife lost their longed-for baby? This was miscarriage number two—did You forget that? Where were You when Jason lost his ability to think rationally and shot a man in broad daylight in front of multiple witnesses? God, my son was trained in covert military activity, and he did this horrifying act in plain*

sight. He totally snapped. Why did You allow this to happen? This
aberrant behavior doesn't match anything about the past history
of my son. He committed his life to You, and I always thought
You protected and guided Your children. But not on a Sunday
afternoon in a Sweet Tomatoes parking lot. Not then.

Since I am not inclined to cynicism, the contemptuous words that so easily flowed off my pen surprised even me.

I thought nothing could touch us without Your permission, so does that
mean You allowed this sickening crime to take place? What kind of a
God would let this stomach-turning, irrational, never-to-be fixed crime to
happen? Were You too busy on the other side of the world? Was this
situation involving my family less important than the global news of the
day? I thought You cared about individual people. I thought You died for
common people like us. I thought You loved us and had a wonderful plan
for our lives. That's what those university campus missionaries always
told me. But I guess we were not special enough to You. The whole thing
makes me sick. I thought I had a firm grip on my theology, but I
really can't find You right now. And this communication is certainly
one-sided, because I can't hear You either. In fact, I never could "hear"
You like other people. You apparently speak to some people out
loud—but not to me! Right now I don't "get" You at all.

Gene and I numbly went through the motions of being alive, but we were mentally and physically dying in our pain and bewilderment while the beliefs that had been the bedrock of our lives—concepts as basic as the love and sovereignty of God— were challenged as never before.

TRYING TO NUMB THE PAIN

One afternoon soon after Jason's arrest, I felt claustrophobic. Gene had left for Florida, and I took a break from working on the financial aspects of the legal process. I hopped on my bicycle and rode north along the St. Clair River. Typically, a bike ride was one of my most enjoyable breaks in the day; I loved to let my hair fly in the wind and to pedal hard enough to work up a sweat. There was nothing more awe-inspiring in my neighborhood than the Blue Water Bridge, arching its way from Port Huron, Michigan, to where it rested on the other side of the mouth of the river in Sarnia, Ontario, Canada, just before the river widened into Lake Huron. It was an Indian summer day, and the warm breeze signaled a final, nostalgic good-bye to beach days and picnics before the cooler temperatures would usher us into another season.

I was hoping I wouldn't run into anyone I knew, but there they were—Steve and Sarah with their son and daughter, on their way home with their boat after the season's final day of fun in the sun. They honked the horn, and with beaming faces, the whole family waved wildly in my direction. Instead of pausing to say hello on a street with absolutely no traffic in sight apart from their truck and my bike, I pedaled furiously while sending a quick wave in their direction. I choked as I thought about how uncomfortable it would be to stop and talk to them. They went to my church. We were friends—well, not close friends, but we knew each other. I couldn't imagine having to make small talk when the news of our son's arrest for murder was burning like acid through my brain and heart.

As I quickly pedaled in the opposite direction and their truck was no longer visible, an unexpected wave of emotion hit me. I couldn't stop my tears. Steve and Sarah had everything. He was a young attorney, and she owned a local business. They had well-behaved, normal, good kids. They were "a perfect little family" who loved God, served in our church, went on mission trips, and gave generously to help meet the needs of others.

From deep inside my soul, I screamed to the wind, *They have my old life! They have happiness! They have a fantastic family and a secure future! They love and trust God, and He's been good to them! We tried to be faithful Christians and to raise our child to be a responsible, caring, compassionate member of society—but he just shot and killed a man. How do things like this happen when you try to do everything right? We read the Bible and prayed. We disciplined our son in appropriate ways. We were supportive and loving parents, but a man is dead. We are facing a trial for first-degree murder. How did Steve and Sarah manage to do everything right—while we obviously did everything wrong?*

I made eye contact with no one as I biked back to the house in record time. After opening the garage, I rolled the bicycle inside and immediately closed the door. I locked all inside doors, trying to place distance between the outside world and my body. If I could shut out the people, perhaps I could shut out the pain. But alone in the house, I found I could finally *be* me—the hurting me. I sobbed until the Kleenex box was empty.

THE NEWS HITS THE FAN

It took two weeks for the news of Jason's arrest to break in our local *Times Herald*. An editor from the paper called three times, trying to get a comment from the grieving parents, but we refused the calls. However, the editor's messages gave us a day's warning that Jason's arrest would be citywide news the next day. I walked around with a knot in my stomach and heaviness on my heart. The next day, the headline took my breath away.

FORMER PORT HURON MAN FACES MURDER CHARGE

A Port Huron native and Naval Academy graduate could face up to life in prison and possibly the death penalty in the shooting death of his wife's ex-husband outside a busy Orlando, Florida, restaurant last month.

Jason Paul Kent, 25, is expected to be charged Tuesday at an Orange County Jail with . . . murder and with shooting into an occupied vehicle.

Authorities said there were a number of eyewitnesses when Mr. Kent allegedly shot and killed Douglas Miller, 35, on October 24.

An Orange County sheriff deputy pulled over Mr. Kent's car immediately after the slaying. Police said he was found with a 9mm that was still warm from firing . . .

Mr. Kent is a 1993 graduate of Port Huron Northern High School, where he was a top athlete and involved in a number of clubs, including National Honor Society, for which he was elected president his senior year.

He was in a Navy diving school in Panama City and ready to transfer to Hawaii with his wife and her two daughters from a previous marriage. The victim, Mr. Miller, objected to the 4,500-mile move . . . [1]

As Gene and I slogged through the days and weeks follow-ing the arrest, it was torturous to go out in public. When we walked into the church lobby, people looked up and acknowl-edged our presence. Then, with eyes swimming in tears, they wept with us, often with no words. One longtime friend said, "What's happened to your family startles us, because if it could happen to you, it could happen to us."

Another friend spoke up: "If for one minute I thought a man with allegations of abuse against him would be allowed unsu-pervised visitation with my children, I would have done the same thing. That could be me—in your son's place at the jail. It's just that those circumstances didn't enter my life." Comments like that certainly didn't justify the crime, but we knew people were trying to encourage us with their honest reactions.

With deep emotion, our good buddy Chuck said, "I feel like it's my fault. I taught J.P. how to shoot a gun on my property when he was a teenager. I shouldn't have done that." Obviously, our son had received a lot of military training since that initial instruction from Chuck, but there was enough blame to go around many times over. No one could make sense out of what had happened.

We were also continuing to grieve deeply for the father, step-mother, and sister of the deceased. I could feel tears well up whenever it hit me: while we were planning a trial for first-degree murder, Douglas Miller's family was planning a funeral.

Two families caught in a bottleneck of suffering. Not know-ing how to reach out to each other.

A GOOD DAY FOR GOSSIP

Then a dreaded day arrived. For years I had gone to the same salon to get my hair colored and cut. The owner of the shop was my hairdresser, and I realized I would either need to stop living—or face life and get my hair colored.

I entered the Chameleon Salon—and all conversation ceased. The sudden silence was startling to me and to everyone else. There are at least fifteen occupied chairs during almost every hour the beauty shop is open, and the noise level is often so loud you can't hear the radio above the animated voices of numerous women. But that day the earth stood still—well, at least it did in that salon—because as I entered the shop, hairdressers and customers, in unison, stopped speaking.

I internalized what I knew they were thinking:

Oh, no! She's here! She's the mother of the murderer—the one we just read about in the paper.

I don't know what to say, so I think I'll just stare at her.

Can you imagine how humiliated and embarrassed she is? I'd never show my face in public again if my son did what her son did.

I wish someone would break this awkward silence so I could go back to gossiping about my neighbor.

In the middle of the interminable awkwardness, I suddenly saw the face of Azam, my Iranian eyebrow plucker. (Well, she takes care of hairy upper lips, too, but that's another story.) Azam saw my misery, recognized the discomfort of the moment, and took me by the hand into her tiny room at the back of the salon. With eyes brimming with tears, she held me tightly and said, "I just don't listen to them. They like to gossip, but they'll get tired of it. They'll talk about someone else next week. I pray for you. I am so sorry about your son. How is he, and how are *you*?"

I remember nothing else about that painful day except the kindness of Azam—a woman who has experienced her own "new kind of normal." Her husband had worked for the shah of Iran before the shah was deposed, and their family finally made it to the United States after a harrowing and circuitous escape through Turkey. She was a woman who knew and understood pain, rejection, being misunderstood, and losing everything. We had often talked about faith, our families, and our beliefs. Azam was building her life on a fresh platform of trust in a new country. Her unwavering courage and tender compassion reminded me that I could learn to trust again too. But how?

MARY'S TRUST

The simple announcement "You're pregnant" usually evokes great emotion. To the couple longing for a child, or to the woman who has struggled through multiple miscarriages while watching her friends give birth to healthy babies, those two words bring renewed hope, positive affirmation, and overwhelming joy. However, to the woman who has been raped, or to the woman who isn't married and feels caught in a situation she doesn't want, the very same words can bring feelings of desperation, self-doubt, and stress—and even questions about why God would allow such a thing to happen.

It had to be hard for Mary to trust God at that moment of the announcement of her upcoming pregnancy, and later when she learned she really *was* expecting a child.

Here's what happened:

> In the sixth month of Elizabeth's pregnancy, God sent the angel Gabriel to the Galilean village of Nazareth to a virgin engaged to be married to a man descended from David. His name was Joseph, and the virgin's name, Mary. Upon entering, Gabriel greeted her: "Good morning! You're beautiful with God's beauty, beautiful inside and out! God be with you." (Luke 1:26–28 MSG)

Hold on a minute. All of us like compliments, but this must have been a startling moment. An angel appears—right in front of Mary—and tells her she is beautiful inside and out. Okay, Gabriel would have gotten my attention too!

> She was thoroughly shaken, wondering what was behind a greeting like that. But the angel assured her, "Mary, you have nothing to fear. God has a surprise for you: You will become pregnant and give birth to a son and call his name Jesus. He will be great, be called 'Son of the Highest.' The Lord God will give him the throne of his father David; He will rule Jacob's house forever—no end, ever, to his kingdom." (vv. 30–33 MSG)

That was no small surprise! And it produced an immediate follow-up question:

> Mary said to the angel, "But how? I've never slept with a man." (v. 34 MSG)

Mary's emotions must have been swirling. At this time in history, fathers usually negotiated marriage arrangements for their daughters when they were still young girls. It was likely that Mary grew up knowing she would marry Joseph and spend the rest of her life with him. Her betrothal to Joseph held much greater significance than today's engagements. A betrothal was legally binding. Even though a couple didn't live together until after the celebration of their marriage, only divorce could break this contractual arrangement.

> The angel answered, "The Holy Spirit will come upon you, the power of the Highest hover over you; Therefore, the child you bring to birth will be called Holy, Son of God. And did you know that your cousin Elizabeth conceived a son, old as she is? Everyone called her barren, and here she is six months pregnant! Nothing, you see, is impossible with God." (vv. 35–37 MSG)

As a mother living in the middle of her own set of shocking circumstances, my "trust meter" rises as I read those words from Gabriel—right out of the Holy Spirit–inspired Scriptures: "Nothing, you see, is impossible with God." Could that mean, if I keep holding on to hope, that one day my son will once again walk in freedom? I *want* to believe it. I *need* to trust God with my son's unknown future in a maximum-security prison where he has a "toe-tag" sentence. (That term is used for someone who will be dead on a slab with a tag on his toe before he ever leaves a Florida state penitentiary.) I want Gabriel's statement to be as true for me as it was for Mary—that I can trust God with my own impossible circumstances and choose to believe that a positive outcome is possible. Perhaps the last chapter isn't written for my son yet?

> And Mary said, "Yes, I see it all now: I'm the Lord's maid, ready to serve. Let it be with me just as you say." Then the angel left her. (v. 38 MSG)

I wish I could be more like Mary every day. My heart longs to trust God the way she did—ready to serve, no matter what the gossip, the criticism, and the misunderstanding from others, in spite of the ache in my soul every time I think of my son. I long to pray with an honest heart, "Be it unto me according to thy word" (Luke 1:38 KJV).

I read her poignant words and think, *Wow. How could she do it? How could she be so wise? So trusting? So surrendered? Was it her youth? Her shock? The result of a lifelong, intimate dependence on God?* It's almost too much to comprehend. I find myself with questions—big questions: *Do I even want to say that to God when the consequences could be so painful? Do I want to get to a place where I give Him that much power? Do I really understand that He already has that power and that my resistance only hurts myself?* Perhaps one day I will learn to trust Him as completely as Mary did.

Karan Gleddie learned trust in a way that gives me hope.

A CRUSHING INJUSTICE

When he proposed to me, my husband confided his hopes and dreams for our new life together. "All I want in life is to own my own ranch someday and raise our family there." This wonderful

Christian man's vision and character were just two of the reasons that I was in love with him.

Lyle and I were married in 1963, and I moved from San Diego to rural Alberta, Canada. Lyle worked on the second-generation ranch where he grew up. At the time, the ranch was owned by Lyle's father and uncle, who were in partnership together.

In 1971, Lyle's uncle decided to sell his share of the ranch. Lyle's father continued to run the ranch with his three sons as a family operation. He put up his half of the ranch as collateral to borrow the money to buy out his brother. The boys' plan was to work on the ranch to pay off the mortgage and receive equal ownership shares in exchange.

My husband and I were ecstatic to see the dream of a lifetime come true. We loved living on the ranch and being involved with the little church in our village. It was a great place to raise our family. With Lyle's parents living on the same property, our three girls would have the privilege of learning from the exam-ple of godly grandparents. Our daughters could rarely pass Grandma's house without stopping for goodies and games.

Unfortunately, the business arrangement for the three broth-ers did not remain in place for long. Two and a half years after the company was started, Lyle's oldest brother sold his shares and pursued other interests. After another two and a half years, Lyle's youngest brother walked off the ranch. He didn't want to spend his time working to pay off the mortgage, and he didn't want to sell his shares. His position was never formally settled.

Left alone with his father on the ranch, Lyle worked hard— sometimes too hard, I thought. During those years we hardly ever took vacations, because all the extra money went to pay the mortgage, upgrade livestock and equipment, and provide a little extra for the years when crops failed or cattle prices were down. I have never seen a man love a job as much as Lyle loved his. He spent many hours reading cattle books, buying bulls, and investigating the right breeding to improve our cattle operation. He read cattle books like I read catalogs.

Although the ranch was demanding, our family was doing well and the Lord seemed to be blessing us and our ministries. We could not imagine our lives being any better. How could we foresee the catastrophe that was looming?

In 1990, Lyle's youngest brother announced that he and his family would be coming back to live on the ranch after a nineteen-year absence. And he intended to return as an equal partner with the right to the full value of his shares. Lyle's father told him that would not be possible, as he was not equally invested in the ranch like Lyle, who had worked all these years. Besides, the ranch would not sustain two families. Lyle's brother responded by saying that he wanted to sell his shares for fair market value, which he felt was his right. We offered to buy them from him, but when our price was less than what he wanted, he became angry.

In late summer 1991, we received a letter of intent informing us that our family had been charged with misappropriation of funds, fixing the books, and poor management. My father-in-law, my husband and I, and our three daughters were all being sued!

I could not believe we were being accused of such horrible actions. I wondered where God was. I believed He knew the injustice we were facing, and I couldn't understand why He was allowing our family to go through this. I asked Him, "Don't we tithe enough, help other people, and serve You?"

Everything was a blur for the next few years. We had to hire two lawyers, one for my father-in-law and the ranch, and one for our family. The stress on the family and the resources of the ranch were astronomical. Nevertheless, we kept going, putting on our "happy faces."

A few years soon became six, then seven, as attorneys burrowed into ranch records. Our lives had been turned upside down and inside out. During this time Lyle had a stroke and struggled to regain full health. My once vibrant father-in-law seemed to age at an alarming rate. But his faith remained strong no matter what happened. Some relatives chose to take sides in the case, while others stepped back so they would not get caught in the middle. We were lonely and hurt, and we often wondered if God really loved us at all.

Many times during those years I would read my Bible and cry. I read the words, but my mind could not take them in. I would sit in church and cry through the worship service. I was confused and did not know what God was planning for us. As I look back, I am reminded of the verse in the Bible that says when we cannot pray, or do not even know what to pray for, the Holy Spirit prays for us in the Father's name, asking for His perfect will for our lives (Rom. 8:26).

In our seventh year of legal proceedings, we were invited to a Bible study group in a nearby town. The people in that group became our lifeline when we thought we couldn't go on. They prayed with us and hugged us—but most of all, they listened to and encouraged us. They became the "face" of God's compassion and unconditional love we so desperately needed.

After nine years of chamber hearings, mediation, and appeals, we finally had a court date and were going to trial. We were scheduled for two weeks of testimonies, examinations, and cross-examinations. We were sure that a trial would vindicate us, put an end to all of this turmoil, and let us get back to a normal life.

Three and a half months after the trial, we received the verdict. My husband was found not guilty. Because of a new law protecting shareholders in Alberta, Canada, however, Lyle's youngest brother was given full value for his shares. Because we had paid for the ranch once, borrowing the money again was not feasible because of our age; we would not live long enough to pay it all off again.

Our hearts were crushed, but something had happened deep inside mine just three months before that sustained me when all of our prayers seemed to be answered with a resounding no. I had agreed to speak for two days at a women's conference. When we received our court dates, we saw that my speaking dates coincided with the first two days of the trial, the days when Lyle would be on the stand. I wanted to cancel the engagements, but my husband insisted I keep them. He said that it would be too hard for me to be in court when he was testifying. But he asked me to pray that the Lord would help him remember and relate the truth correctly.

As Lyle left for court and I left for two days of speaking, I was heartbroken. I was not sure if I could pull myself together. How could I tell women about God's great love for them when I wasn't even sure that He loved me? I felt abandoned and confused. Driving down the highway, I was sobbing, begging the Lord to help me. I felt I didn't have anything to give these women.

I pulled over to the side of the road, still weeping, and

noticed that the car radio had been on. At that moment I heard Charles Stanley say, "The sovereignty of God is the pillow we lay our head upon." I knew those words were for me. God had reminded me that no matter what happened, He was in control and I could trust Him for this journey, wherever it led us. As I pulled back onto the road, I was filled with a new confidence that God was with me, and I felt secure that His plans are bigger, wider, and higher than I could ever imagine or hope for. For the first time in so long, I *felt* these life-sustaining truths in my broken heart.

After the verdict was announced, the ranch sold within three months—at a time when land and cattle were both highly valued. Two months after the sale, my godly father-in-law passed into eternity to see the Savior he trusted and loved. He had prayed that the Lord would allow him to live long enough to make sure his son, Lyle, would be all right. God answered that prayer.

The public auction for the machinery and three generations of antiques was held on my husband's sixtieth birthday. We had spent twenty-nine years on the ranch, raised our family, and formed a wonderful community of friends. Now strangers were carrying off our memories.

Hebrews 11:8 became a sweet comfort to me. It reads, "It was by faith that Abraham obeyed when God called him to leave home and go to another land that God would give him as his inheritance. He went without knowing where he was going" (NLT).

I could never have imagined that God would bring me back to California after all those years in Canada. After our son-in-law was deployed to Iraq, God downsized us and moved us to northern California to encourage our daughter. I have always known that God would take my speaking ministry in a different direction, but I was never sure when or how. Living in California, I have more time to write and opportunities to speak to women about God's unconditional love and faithfulness.

Sometimes we feel sad when we drive by ranching communities and think about our old life, wondering what things would be like if we were still living on our property. Some days I feel anxious, wishing God would hurry and let me see the whole picture for my life, but I realize that patience and waiting and trusting Him are characteristics that God is still working on in my life.

My husband and I are practicing walking in faith, secure in knowing that God's plans are bigger, wider, and higher than we could ever imagine. He holds us in the palm of His hand, shelters us from the storms, calms our souls, and brings peace to our hearts. We are living a new kind of normal, but we have found that "Jesus is enough" is not just a cliché for us. His character, rather than our own hopes and dreams, is the bedrock of our lives.[2]

TRUST LOOKS FORWARD

Will I trust my son's future to God—even if he is stalked in the prison yard by violent sex offenders, even if he is never granted an end-of-sentence date, even if every free weekend for the rest of my life I can only see him inside the razor wire? It all comes back to God and me—and there's a battle for my mind and heart.

I think I understand what trust is, and I demand it of others, but what is it *really*? The dictionary says *trust* is "assured reliance on the character, ability, strength, or truth of someone or something, one in which confidence is placed, dependence on something future or contingent: HOPE."[3] It was an epiphany for me to discover that even in the dictionary, the words *hope* and *trust* are used together.

Recently my friend Sandra Aldrich reminded me of the details of her own most challenging days. I first met Sandra at Maranatha Bible and Missionary Conference in Muskegon, Michigan. She and her husband, Don, were high school teachers, which allowed them to have summers off. They had a summer cottage at the conference center on Lake Michigan, and they loved entertaining friends, dreaming about a secure future, and planning which universities their children would attend. All that was changed as the doctor murmured, "I'm sorry. I'm so very sorry." Don was diagnosed with terminal cancer. He and Sandra were the parents of two young children—Jay, ten, and Holly, eight.

Letting go of her husband and her "perfect-family" status involved copious tears and constantly holding out empty hands to the One who promised never to leave nor forsake His children. Sandra remembers unabashedly questioning God's timing.

"I remember the exact spot on Lake Harbor Drive as I drove home from the hospital after Don's original diagnosis—where I told God how wrong the situation was and reminded Him of all the people who needed Don (even beyond Jay, Holly, and me). But in the middle of my complaints, I burst into tears as I realized I was giving orders to the God of the universe. When I could talk again, I said aloud, 'I'm broken. Here are the pieces. Do what You want.'"

Sandra's prayer sounds to me a lot like Mary's response: "Be it unto me according to thy word." From that point on, Sandra's prayers were pleas for healing, but also for strength for the day-to-day process—especially as Don surrendered medical and household decisions to her. Often she had only enough strength to say, "Help, Lord. Please help."

When she gave her children the news of their dad's diagnosis, Jay asked if his dad was going to die. After she answered, "The doctors say he will," Holly asked, "Does God love Daddy?" Sandra answered, "Yes. Very much."

Holly then asked, "If God loves Daddy, won't He make him well?" Holly's mom answered that God could heal their dad, but He would be with them no matter what happened. "I'm not sure I handled that discussion very well," Sandra says. "After all, I'd never had to explain God's sovereignty to children before."

When Sandra came home from the hospital to tell her children that their dad had died, she saw the verse on the kitchen counter that Jay had been memorizing for Sunday school: "But my God shall supply all your need according to his riches in glory by Christ Jesus" (Phil. 4:19 KJV). In that moment, Sandra made a decision to trust that truth. It didn't reduce the intensity of her family's great loss, but it comforted her. "My mind flashed back to Don's words to me on the morning before he died: 'Just remember, San, the Lord never promised us an easy road, but He did promise to always be with us on that road.' In time, I chose to grab God's hand as I kept putting one foot in front of the other—even when my heart was heavy and the loneliness was overwhelming."

Two weeks after Don died, Holly asked her mom, "When we prayed, didn't God listen?" That night, Sandra had to explain how bad things are often part of life. And knowing the propensity we all have to compare ourselves to others, she wanted her daughter to get the comparison going in the right direction. "I reminded Holly of my grandfather who died when my dad was two, and of the neighbor who had died in a car accident the week before. His wife was pregnant with a baby he would never hold. My response may not have made complete sense to a child, but I needed to remind myself that life isn't always fair—and we're not home yet."

Jay and Holly are grown now. How Sandra wishes that Don could have been here for their graduations and their weddings! "He would have been a wonderful grandpa," Sandra says. "But regret looks backward, and trust looks forward. I choose trust."[4]

Author Nancy Guthrie says, "Trusting God when the miracle does not come, when the urgent prayer gets no answer, when there is only darkness—this is the kind of faith God values perhaps most of all."[5]

Will I learn to pray Mary's prayer honestly, "Be it unto me according to thy word"? Will I walk into the hair salon next time with my head held high and a smile on my face, not minding if people gossip about me and my family because I know that no matter what, I can choose to trust Him?

Deep down I know that in Mary's story and in mine, *nothing* is impossible with God. And that gives me hope.

GOD'S POWER IN YOUR
NEW KIND OF NORMAL

At some point in our lives, most of us will face a faith test. It is that moment in time when what we have always believed about who God is and what He allows to happen in our lives intersects with the reality of our experience—a head-on collision between our faith and the hard facts of an impossible situation. It's a time when we sometimes question the goodness of God because we are having difficulty understanding what "trust" looks like. On the surface, nothing makes sense. We relive the scene of an accident, or we remember the details of watching a loved one die—too early. We mentally revisit the hospital room when the doctor tactfully reports that our newborn baby has a serious birth defect.

Over time, we wrestle with the question, is God trustworthy? The outward appearance of the situation does not indicate that God intervened in our circumstances. Will we cut and run from our relationship with God, or will we rely on Him and believe His character is still good?

1. When you were growing up, who was the person you trusted the most? What built that trust relationship? Did it remain intact, or did something happen to destroy the trust? Did your early trust in a person influence your ability or inability to trust God as an adult?

2. How do you define trust today? How does trust impact your daily decisions—for yourself, and for your family and close friends?

3. Proverbs 3:5–6 says, "Trust in the LORD with all your heart and lean not on your own understanding; in all your ways acknowledge him, and he will make your paths straight." In your experience, what does that passage mean? Has there been a situation in your life when you made a decision based on your own understanding instead of allowing God

to reveal a clarified plan for the future as you rested in His wisdom? Your response might not have involved a major life-altering decision, but it may have been a time when you wanted to fix a problem that wasn't turning out the way you anticipated. What was the result?

4. Karan Gleddie's moving story deals with betrayal by a family member. Have you ever been in a situation when the people you thought you could trust the most failed you during a time when you were emotionally, financially, or spiritually needy? If so, how did you respond? If your own situation did not have a favorable resolution, how did you hold on to trust in God? (It's okay to say you are still struggling!)

5. Earlier in this chapter, you read Brennan Manning's unique perspective on trust: "Ruthless trust ultimately comes down to this: faith in the person of Jesus and hope in His promise. In spite of all disconcerting appearances, we stare down death without nervousness and anticipate resurrection solely because Jesus has said, 'You have my word on it.'"[6] How does the power of the Resurrection impact the state of your mind and heart when circumstances tempt you to question what God has allowed to happen in your life?

6. What would you like to express to God as a result of reading this chapter? As honestly as you can, write a prayer that expresses your questions regarding trust issues, along with your affirmation of what you are clinging to in your quest to trust God, whether or not you can see the next chapter in your own new kind of normal.

three
A PROLONGED JOURNEY

When I Desperately Want Relief from Unrelenting Reality . . .
I CHOOSE PERSEVERANCE

HOW DO WE GET TO THE MORNING,
TO THE SUNSHINE, TO THE JOY?
THERE IS ONLY ONE WAY. BY WAITING FOR IT.
WE CAN'T HURRY THE DAWN,
NO MATTER HOW ANXIOUSLY WE PACE THE FLOOR
OR HOW IMPATIENTLY WE WATCH THE CLOCK.
AND SO THE QUESTION IS NOT DO WE WAIT
OR NOT WAIT, BECAUSE WAITING IS ALL WE CAN DO.
THE QUESTION IS, HOW WILL WE WAIT?
WILL WE WAIT WELL . . . OR WILL WE WAIT POORLY?
—KEN GIRE

The woman pushed through the crowd to get to me. "But you forgot to tell us the end of the story," she said imploringly. "You know, the part about when your son was released from prison." I was at the book table autographing copies of *When I Lay My Isaac Down* following my presentation on our journey with our son. Several women leaned closer, trying to listen in on my response. I had a wave of claustrophobia as they invaded my personal space, hoping for more of the story than I had already shared publicly.

"Ma'am," I said politely, "you must have missed the part of my presentation when I said the conviction was for first-degree murder, and the sentence, due to the mandatory minimums in the state of Florida, is life without the possibility of parole."

"Yes, I heard that," she said, "but what about an appeal?"

"That was denied one year after his conviction," I stated as calmly as possible.

"Well, what are you going to do next?" she countered. "Can't he be freed on bail while you work on more appeals? He's not a threat to society." The group of listening women came in even closer, stifling my breathing space. I could feel myself perspiring under the watchful eyes of the growing crowd who wanted to hear my answer. It seemed impossible for this woman to believe that when someone is convicted and sentenced for murdering a man he believed was abusive to his stepdaughters, the prison doors are permanently closed. The key is thrown away. The judge's gavel falls, and the sentence is forever.

"Well," she spouted, "it's just not fair. It's not right that he should get the same sentence as the Green River Killer who stalked, raped, and murdered more than forty women. Your son believed he was protecting two little girls from potential abuse." Finally, she realized that she couldn't change the result of the trial by continuing to talk, so she hugged me awkwardly and mumbled, "You need a miracle."

Yes, we did. And we still do.

A SERIES OF LONG WAITS

I have never waited well. As the firstborn of six preacher's kids, I was used to functioning in a very busy, highly productive, schedule-oriented household. As I grew older and entered adulthood, I prided myself on planning ahead to avoid idle time. I carried my daily planner with me to the offices of doctors and dentists. While other people browsed through magazines or watched television, I wrote thank-you notes and worked on projects I brought with me. The following expressions did *not* describe the way I waited: biding my time, cooling my heels, or marking time. I loved being productive and enjoyed helping other people learn how to reclaim time that was often lost in the waiting rooms of everyday life.

When our son was arrested, we began a series of totally unexpected waiting periods that changed my perspective on the subject of perseverance. In an early stage of our journey, Gene and I experienced:

- Waiting for updates from Jason's attorney
- Waiting in long visitation lines at the jail
- Waiting for word on a potential plea bargain
- Waiting for a trial date (We went through two and a half years and seven postponements before the trial eventually took place.)
- Waiting for digitized calls from the jail indicating our son was making contact with us (We could not initiate those calls.)

- Waiting to physically touch our son without a Plexiglas window between us (Jason was held in the county jail in Orlando for two and a half years while awaiting trial. Only after his eventual conviction were we finally allowed to hug our son—in a Central Florida prison.)

- Waiting on any sign from God that He was aware of—or cared about—our situation

I could hardly bear lingering in a situation that lacked resolution. I wanted to investigate all of the possible options, pick the best one, form a plan of action, and move ahead to a positive outcome. But our waiting wasn't like that. Our waiting was sweaty, uncomfortable, nerve-wracking, headache producing, and exasperating. I wanted to anticipate a favorable resolution and to facilitate the process of attaining the end result as speedily as possible. But that was not my "new normal."

What I could not convey at a book table in a church lobby to a well-meaning woman inquiring about "the end of the story" was the long road we had already traveled. Not only had Jason's appeal been denied, but the appeal to the appeal had been denied. So we scraped several thousand more dollars together and paid a retainer for yet another attorney and went to work on the 3.850 motion. (That's legal terminology for the ineffective counsel statute.) And after interminable months that had grown into another three and a half years of waiting on postconviction statutes and motions (many of which sounded like Greek to me), the 3.850 motion was rejected. Numerous letters arrived from the new attorney, with similar terminology in each one:

- We continue to monitor your case for progress. No new activity has occurred on the motion.

- To date, the Court is still taking our Motion and the State's Response under consideration, and has provided us no timeframe with which to expect a response.

- In the case of *State of Florida v. Jason Kent*: We are pursuing the appeal of the trial court's denial of our Rule 3.850 motion without an evidentiary hearing.

- Enclosed please find a copy of the Court's Order Denying First Amended Motion for Post-Conviction Relief.

And finally, almost nine months after that door closed, an envelope arrived in our mailbox from the attorney stating:

- Enclosed please find a copy of the Decision from the Fifth District Court of Appeals affirming the lower Court opinion on the 3.850 Appeal from the Circuit Court for Orange County. At this time we will await a mandate and proceed to file a Petition for Habeas Corpus on your behalf.

At first, when I read the word "affirming" in the above letter, I got excited. I was used to reading words like *dismissed, rejected,* and *denied.* Then I read the letter again and realized what was being affirmed was a lower court's previous rejection.

I looked at Gene and screamed: "I have a master's degree! I am an educated woman, and I speak internationally to intelligent people—but I can't begin to understand the wording in these rulings! How do people with no education and no financial resources ever make it through this unending maze of legalese? This is maddening!"

Even as I yelled, I realized Gene was as frustrated as I was with the endless wait and with the numerous ways attorneys and governmental officials could type the word that meant only one thing—*rejection!*

HURRICANES AND HEARTACHES

Gene and I were not the only ones with our lives on hold. Jason's new family was waiting too. One day I was in a clothing store with my daughter-in-law and the girls, and all four of us were hunting for bargains. On the sale rack was an evening gown, complete with satin, lace, and an irresistible price tag. It was in my daughter-in-law's favorite color—purple. Her seven-year-old pulled it off the rack and enthusiastically tugged at her mother's arm. "Mom, this dress is so pretty. It would look good on you. Let's buy it so you can be beautiful when Daddy comes home." A piece of my heart died as I saw the fallen look on her mom's face.

Later, as I tucked my younger granddaughter in for the night, she prayed the same prayer she voiced every time I sat at the edge of her bed for her nighttime ritual: " . . . and Lord, please help Daddy to come home soon. Amen." My heart ached. I wondered how long these precious little girls would still believe God was a good God and that He answered prayer if their stepfather never came home again.

Following Jason's placement in a maximum-security facility, we helped his wife and her daughters move to a little town within driving distance of the prison. Life for them was challenging on multiple levels, but they were doing their best to creatively figure out how to find a new kind of normal, with regular prison visits, letters, and phone calls to keep communication alive.

Then came Hurricane Charley in the summer of 2004, ripping into Punta Gorda, and as a powerful and destructive category 4 hurricane, coming inland—right through the prison where Jason was located, and directly through the town where our daughter-in-law and our grandchildren lived. My husband and I flew to Orlando and drove south, hoping to help with some of the hurricane cleanup, wondering why our Florida family should have to go through these personal and financial challenges, in addition to everything else they had already endured. It made no sense.

Then, only three weeks later, Hurricane Frances ripped through the state with a one-two punch. Jason's family evacuated just before the storm and set up a tent in a campground, far north of the path of the hurricane. When they returned home, our daughter-in-law called with a report on the damages. More water had leaked through the roof that had been damaged during the first hurricane, and now there was additional damage to the carpet and the walls. Our daughter-in-law is a licensed artist, and the exquisite wall murals she had painstakingly created in her daughters' bedrooms were now on soaked, warped wallboard. She didn't know what could be salvaged.

For days we didn't receive a phone call from our son, indicating that his prison was without electricity. I fought to hold on to hope, but my unrelenting reality was another story. In the middle of fear, heartache, and uncertainty, the enemy came at me with his cold-blooded taunts:

Your son is in danger and you can't contact him. He could be beaten or raped and you have no way of getting accurate information. You can't help him.

His marriage can't possibly survive a separation of this magnitude and a sentence of this severity.

The laws will never change. Your son is doomed to live out the rest of his life behind prison walls.

God must not love you or He wouldn't put you through this torment.

Gene and I began to notice a deep sadness in our daughter-in-law. Her smile was gone, along with her former joyful anticipation of holidays and family gatherings. We were used to talking to her on the phone almost daily, but there were now longer lapses in between the conversations she had with us. Then we sensed an emotional distancing from us that we believed was triggered by multiple losses—emotional and personal stresses from the trial, the loss of her husband to lifelong incarceration, and the unanticipated additional challenges of the hurricanes.

Then we discovered, quite unexpectedly, that she was visiting Jason less frequently. We understood. She had hurricane cleanup to do, and immediately after the last hurricane, Jason and other maximum-security inmates were moved to a prison near Miami—a seven-hour round trip from his wife and stepchildren—so minimum-security prisoners could be moved into Hardee to help with hurricane cleanup. It was only natural that J.P. and his wife could no longer see each other *every* weekend. But when Christmas came that year and we suggested to our daughter-in-law that we fly into Orlando, pick up her and the girls, and drive several hours south to visit Jason together, she told us she didn't want to go. This unexpected response to potential Christmas plans provided an unwanted foreshadowing of a new chapter in our lives.

There are moments when my mother heart screams out loud, "Enough already! I can take *no more*. God, do you love us? Do You care? Do You have a statute of limitations on the amount of pain one family is allowed to endure?"

But when I look beyond the "me" part of my struggle, I remember that Mary had an only son too. Her son was sinless. Mine is not. But she watched her son suffer and experienced the agony of desperate times and unthinkable family circumstances.

In my rational moments, I know I must persevere when there is no hope of a favorable result; it is the right thing to do as a Christian parent. I know a better day is coming—a day my son will walk in freedom. I pray it's during this lifetime, but I have no promise of that. Until then, I choose to release my controlling grip on my circumstances for another day, to release my son to my heavenly Father, and to persevere.

MARY'S CHALLENGES

When I look closely at the period in which Mary the mother of Jesus grew up, I realize there were probably several times in her life when she longed for relief from the challenging circumstances she encountered.

As a teenager, she lived in occupied Palestine—not only before she got pregnant but throughout her life. The unrelenting reality she faced was political oppression and crushing taxation that reduced families like hers to poverty.

The Law of Moses set out two alternative tithes (one in

Leviticus and one in Deuteronomy), but by the time of Mary, the priest running the temple in Jerusalem had combined the taxes, so people were supposed to pay roughly 20 percent of their income to maintain the sacrifices and political system at the temple, as well as funding for local village priests. There were thousands of these local priests, and Zechariah was one of them. They looked forward to their occasional opportunities to go to the temple and participate in the sacrifices, but most of the time they lived in villages and taught the people.

Some Jews thought the double tithe was fair to support the work of God, while others thought the temple priests were corrupt. But on top of this steep tax, the Romans also required the Jews to pay taxes to support the empire—and they didn't make the tax in Judea lower than the tax in Egypt, in spite of the fact that the Jews were already paying 20 percent in Judea. Jews loathed giving that money to the Romans because it represented how "not free" they were. It is estimated that the total tax burden was between 30 and 40 percent of their income, and possibly higher.[1] That meant debt was a major problem. Most average people were in serious debt to loan sharks and/or landowners and aristocrats.

As Gene and I faced the rising legal expenses of Jason's trial and subsequent appeals, we wondered if we would ever be debt-free again. Since the release of *When I Lay My Isaac Down*, I have heard from hundreds of readers who have loved ones who are incarcerated—and part of their unrelenting reality is the gigantic burden of legal expenses. Two weeks ago, I stood in the exit line at the prison, waiting to go through the heavy, loud double doors between the visitation area and freedom. Nancy was behind me, and we often chatted when we were at the facility on the same day. She had been introduced to her incarcerated husband through mutual friends. Nancy and Jim had a lot in common and fell in love during their visits at the prison—and that's where they were married.

Now, eight years later, with a marriage that has yet to be consummated with any physical intimacy, she said, "I feel like my ability to persevere has reached an all-time low. Every time I pay Jim's attorney, I assume he is working on the case, but I have no proof of that. Then I get another bill and ask what this one's for. I feel like I have fallen into a hopeless money pit that I will never climb out of. Don't we have enough stress just dealing with his incarceration? This growing financial strain is breaking me, little by little—and there are days when I feel like throwing in the towel on the attorney and on the marriage."

Financial challenges aren't only in the form of high taxes and legal expenses. Perhaps you can identify with the economic strain of:

- A child's disability
- The death of a spouse
- A divorce
- A change from being a two-income family to a one-income family
- The loss (or downsizing) of a job or ministry position
- An unexpected diagnosis from the doctor
- An accident that causes permanent physical challenges

- Education expenses for your children
- Adult parents who need assisted living and medical care

The list is endless, and you can fill in the blank for yourself regarding a time (maybe even now) when you have had to persevere in the middle of financial challenges.

In Mary's day, in addition to great financial challenges, there were no doubt daily humiliations by an occupying army, accompanied by social instability as some of the Jews agitated for revolt. There were also ferocious debates among Jewish factions as to how to live as a good Jew. We know Mary cared about the social, political, and economic situation, because that's what she talked about when she praised God for the coming Messiah in Luke 1:

> Oh, how my soul praises the Lord.
>> How my spirit rejoices in God my Savior!
> For he took notice of his lowly servant girl,
>> and from now on all generations will call me blessed.
> For the Mighty One is holy,
>> and he has done great things for me.
> He shows mercy from generation to generation
>> to all who fear him.
> His mighty arm has done tremendous things!
>> He has scattered the proud and haughty ones.
> He has brought down princes from their thrones
>> and exalted the humble.
> He has filled the hungry with good things
>> and sent the rich away with empty hands. (vv. 46–53 NLT)

God's plan to fill the hungry with good things and send the rich away empty wasn't just metaphorical for Mary. Like the rest of her people, she yearned for justice and basic security. I daresay she thought her son was going to bring the political kingdom of God that most Jews expected, because in verse 52 she says, "He has brought down rulers from their thrones." And she was so confident that God would deliver on His Old Testament promises that she sang this song in the *past* tense, as though the blessings had already happened.

One of my brave friends understands this level of perseverance.

A DIFFERENT KIND OF LOVE STORY

I'll never forget the first time I laid eyes on Rex. He strode into the room sporting a turquoise shirt, jeans, and the coolest pair of cowboy boots I'd ever seen. When my girlfriend introduced us, his gentle blue eyes locked with my brown ones, and I thought, *I'm going to marry that guy!*

Two years later, we stood at the altar of the Baptist church I'd grown up in and promised to love each other forever. As far as my new hubby and I were concerned, it was a "till death do us part" kind of deal. But I had no idea how hard it would eventually become to keep that promise.

Within two years, we brought our firstborn son home from the hospital. Two years later we had another baby boy, and a few years after that another. We were a family. It was all I'd ever wanted. Having grown up with an angry, dysfunctional father, I thought Rex's kind manner and generosity were almost too good to be true.

As years went by, I have to admit there were times I felt a bit overwhelmed by the overabundance of male hormones reverberating around our house. Still I was blissfully happy. We were Christians involved in all kinds of church-related activities—children's camps, youth group, choir, Bible studies, discipleship training, and volleyball—lots of volleyball. Our boys enjoyed all kinds of sports. I must have warmed thousands of bleachers and yelled myself hoarse hundreds of times as I cheered them on from the sidelines. Seems to me the teen years were the best. Our house was always full of bright, happy, guitar-playing, cookie-munching, milk-guzzling teenagers. I can't remember a serious problem as long as our sons lived under our roof. But when our oldest son left home for college, it was a huge transition—especially for Rex.

He became quiet, withdrawn, sullen. He had a radical change of personality that didn't get better. When our second son left home, it became even more noticeable. Almost every day, as soon as Rex got home from work, he'd change into something comfortable and go outside. I'd watch through the kitchen window as he wandered around the backyard. Sometimes he'd pull a few weeds from the lawn or pick a tomato from one of the vines he'd planted. I wondered what was wrong. I asked him about it and at times suggested he talk to our pastor or a counselor. "Oh, it's nothing!" he'd answer. "Just miss my boys."

I knew this problem was bigger than empty-nest syndrome, but what could it be? What could have gone wrong? I found myself thinking through the years we'd shared, searching for some clue, some misstep that had changed the direction of our marriage. Surely there was more to our relationship than raising children. Besides that, we still had one chick in the nest.

One day as I pondered all this, I found myself smiling when I remembered how we refused to let our kids rob us of our intimacy. At times Rex would playfully quip, "I want to know you—in the *biblical* sense of the word." Then he would spin me around into a big bear hug and hold me close. Sometimes I was the one to suggest some adult "knowing." That's all it took for us to pack our bags, including some of my prettiest lingerie, hire a babysitter, and head out of town. We'd check into a hotel, go out for dinner, then spend the night making love and "spooning" in bed till sunrise. After breakfast we'd head back home, ready to face the challenges of parenting. Romantic getaways happened frequently—a warm tradition that began early on and lasted throughout our marriage. Now I knew there was something wrong, but I was certain of one thing. My Rex could not be having an affair. Our "affair" had always been and would always be a love affair with each other.

Nevertheless, Rex continued to be introspective, moody, refusing to talk. I prayed like I'd never prayed before—facedown on the floor, on my knees before sunrise, as I walked the country roads near our house, with buckets of tears, and with my own share of introspection. Had I failed in some way? Did Rex get lost in the hectic pace of our family life? Had I ignored his needs while doting on my boys? Why didn't I pay more attention when I noticed his interest in spiritual matters wane? Was there anything I could have done about it?

As I dealt with my own raw emotions, I realized how much we'd drifted apart—emotionally, spiritually, physically—settling into a routine that fostered independence. We usually ate dinner in front of the TV. Afterward, while our youngest son did homework or talked on the phone with friends, I would find a book to read and go to bed early. Rex would retreat to our study, boot up the computer, and surf the Web until long after I had gone to sleep.

One evening as I tossed and turned in bed, thinking about the gaping chasm between us, I decided to try, one more time, to talk to Rex. I swallowed a rising lump in my throat, pulled on a robe, and headed downstairs to the study.

When I rounded the corner, my heart stopped. The graphic pornographic scene on the computer screen made me grab my stomach and run out of the room. Rex bolted up the stairs behind me. He sank onto our bed and muttered, "Close the door."

I did as he said and then turned to face him. "How big a problem is this?" I sobbed out the words and waited.

It seemed like an eternity before he finally spoke. "It's big!"

For over an hour he vomited out details. Details that made my head spin and literally broke my heart. What he revealed was much more than an occasional viewing of nude bodies. His problems were deep-seated, core issues that called into question his basic beliefs and values, matters that left me deeply wounded and confused. I demanded specifics. What kind of movies had he rented? What magazines? Which Web sites? Neither of us slept that night. We talked for hours and cried until there were no more tears.

The next morning after Rex left for work, I became my own private detective. I really don't understand why I reacted this way or whether it was helpful. I only know I wanted full disclosure. I drove to the video store and picked up a movie he'd mentioned. At a nearby convenience store, I purchased a pornographic magazine. Back at home, I watched the movie, read the magazine, and searched Web sites. The more I investigated, the sicker I became. Once I ran to the bathroom and threw up. What kind of man had Rex become? Or worse, had he always had a secret life? With all our teasing about knowing each other, had I *known* him at all? I felt deceived, manipulated, violated. Rex hadn't had an affair. He'd had thousands of them. With women who had perfect bodies and huge sexual appetites. How could I compete with that? After a few days, I decided to see a counselor. Rex found a counselor of his own.

The next few months were agonizing. I learned more things I didn't want to know—about his family of origin, secrets he'd hidden since childhood, lies he had told since the day we first met. Too much information turned my world upside down.

It was during this turbulent time that I learned what it means to persevere. In our Bible study group, we looked up the meaning of the word and discovered that it described a person who would not swerve from her deliberate purpose or lose faith even in the greatest test or suffering. Even though there were times when I wanted to get in my car and drive as fast and as far as I could, how could I leave Rex, the love of my life? How could I disillusion our children? I decided to stay put, to work on our problems, to abide under the trial. Somehow, even though I couldn't see past the present pain, I knew God would bless my obedience.

As I struggled with so many things I didn't understand, I held on to what I knew for sure. Jesus would never leave or forsake me. He became dearer to me than any earthly tie. He literally became the lover of my soul, my closest friend. Strengthened by His presence, I was able to take a big step of faith. One evening as Rex and I sat on the sofa in our living room, I turned, knelt before him, and looked up into his face. He seemed so broken, so ashamed, I couldn't hold back tears. "Rex," I sobbed, "I forgive you. Let's begin all over again."

"I'll never do it again," he sobbed as he pulled me close. "You can trust me."

I'd never heard him speak more sincerely. And I know at that moment, he meant every word. But the truth is, he did do it again. And again. And again. And again. And again. Sometimes he'd successfully fight off the temptation for a few months. But sooner or later, he would fall. With every failure I took a big hit myself. I was losing respect for my husband and began to wonder if I loved him at all. My counselor helped me realize that for Rex this was more than a temptation; he was an addict. It helped some for me to think of him as "sick." Still, in the throes of his addiction, our whole lives were affected—the way he touched me, the words he said, the way he managed his time, how he handled his relationship with our boys. I felt as if my whole life was falling apart. And, indeed, in many ways it was.

While all this had been taking place, our boys had grown into men. Men with their own set of problems. During college, one of our sons experimented with a powerful drug. The friends who offered it to him called it "recreational," but, as it turned out, there was nothing fun about it. Quickly addicted by this substance, our precious boy spiraled downward. Eventually he was arrested for possession of a controlled substance and incarcerated, serving eighteen months in prison. Another son became addicted to alcohol and has been in and out of rehab as he tries to tame the monster that dominates his life. Our youngest battles depression as he strives to be the perfect one, the redeemer of our clan. Our sons have known periods of perfect freedom—extended periods filled with joy. They have married and had children. But, like their dad, their addictions haunt them. Relapses have affected their marriages and hurt their children.

We took a giant step forward one day in a family counseling session, when Rex took a huge personal risk. Believing that before a problem can be solved it must be brought to the light, he admitted his addiction to our children. The confession was gut-wrenchingly real and candid. As difficult as it must have been for Rex, it opened the door for our boys to talk about their addictions. In recent years, as we continue to confront the destructive behavior patterns in our family with authentic dialogue, we've been able to include our older grandchildren in the circle. We're determined to break the cycle of addiction and oppression before it's passed on to our third and fourth generations.

There are times when the pressures and problems our family has had to face seem overwhelming. Still I am determined to live by faith, not by my feelings. The men in my life are basically good. They are handsome, fun-loving, deep-thinking, kind-hearted guys, but they are men with one huge problem. Every day of their lives they have to fight the good fight of faith, pay attention to intense spiritual warfare, and make right choices. Meanwhile I cling to Christ and with dogged determination choose not to be swallowed up by the circumstances that tend to swamp us. In fact, in the midst of our personal chaos, I began pursuing a long-cherished dream—that of becoming a writer. Today I'm the author of several books and articles. I travel throughout the United States speaking at conferences and retreats, teach Bible studies, and mentor younger women.

I believe we find our true self in the midst of suffering, pain, and sorrow, not in the absence of it. Don't ask me why this is so; it just is. Maybe it's because trials reveal the shallowness in us or teach us to depend on a power greater than ourselves. Or because it dims the attractions the world has to offer and casts a bright light onto spiritual realities. I tend to think it's because we find in our suffering a point of identity with Jesus the Christ, the One who suffered in our place. There is no closer fellowship with our Lord than "the fellowship of his sufferings." It's a place of "knowing" more intimate, more precious than any human connection. In this place, He reveals Himself and opens up spiritual truth.

One day in my personal Bible study time, I read, "Blessed is a man who perseveres under trial, for once he has been approved, he will receive the crown of life which the Lord has promised to those who love Him" (James 1:12 NASB). As I studied the deeper meaning of some of the words in this verse, I discovered that the "crown" mentioned is the victor's crown, like one presented to the winner of an Olympic race. And it doesn't just mean we will wear that crown in heaven. Oh, no! We will celebrate victory every day of our lives, beginning right here, right now. And that victorious celebration will last throughout the eternal ages in the presence of God our Father, in intimate oneness with Jesus our Lord.

I've known inexpressible joy, even while experiencing excruciating pain, as I have lived out my days here on earth. And I have peace that is beyond human understanding. I think that's possible because I know I'm in the center of God's perfect will. Today I actually enjoy being with the men in my life. I focus on their many good qualities. We laugh and play and pray and talk, talk, talk. When a crisis comes, we cling to each other, to God, and to the truth we know. We are supporting each other with an imperfect but abiding love. And that gives me hope.

Author Jan Frank says, "Waiting in hope means that we rest our faith and expectation, not in what God will do for us, but on God who is our hope and expectation."[2] It means choosing to live out the truth of Micah 7:7: "But as for me, I watch in hope for the LORD, I wait for God my Savior; my God will hear me."

WAITING WITH HOPE

Mary finished her song with these words:

> He has helped his servant Israel
> and remembered to be merciful.
> For he made this promise to our ancestors,
> to Abraham and his children forever.
> (Luke 1:54–55 NLT)

This story is remarkable when you realize how long her unrelenting, imperfect and challenging reality went on. Think about it from Mary's perspective. It was thirty years until Jesus started His ministry, followed by three hopeful years of His visible work on earth; then came His death, and three days later—His resurrection. But still the Romans didn't go away. Her people were still poor, still oppressed. She had to persevere in the already-but-not-yet of God's kingdom, trusting that what she sang about as a teenager was already happening and would someday happen fully.

That's what I call persevering until the miracle happens! I hope I will be that strong—even if my son doesn't walk in freedom during my lifetime. Will I sing praises to God as I wait for my miracle? Will I reiterate what I know to be true about His Word and His promises, persevering in the face of harsh and unrelenting circumstances, even singing songs of worship and praise to a God who, as far as I can determine, has not answered my prayers? Or will I give in to depression, discouragement, and hopelessness?

Author Ben Patterson says, "To hear God's promise . . . is to hear something that perhaps no one else around us can hear. It is to feel ourselves begin to tap our toes and move gently to the beat of the music, perhaps to the bewilderment of those watching us. The music we hear is the music of God's future. Hope is hearing the tune; faith is to dance to it now."[3]

I long for the faith of Mary. I'd like to have the perseverance of my honest friend who is married to Rex. Because of their examples, I feel stronger. They help me visualize an eternal perspective that sees beyond the unrelenting reality of today. I want to anticipate a positive future even when I see no evidence of movement in an affirmative direction. I'm not there yet, but I'm trying to be honest about my struggle and I'm memorizing the following Scripture because it reminds me that perseverance has a big reward!

Do you see what this means—all these pioneers who blazed the way, all these veterans cheering us on? It means we'd better get on with it. Strip down, start running—and never quit! No extra spiritual fat, no parasitic sins. Keep your eyes on Jesus, who both began and finished this race we're in. Study how he did it. Because he never lost sight of where he was headed—that exhilarating finish in and with God—he could put up with any-thing along the way: Cross, shame, whatever. And now he's there, in the place of honor, right alongside God. When you find yourselves flagging in your faith, go over that story again, item by item, that long litany of hostility he plowed through. That will shoot adrenaline into your souls! (Heb. 12:1–3 MSG)

GOD'S POWER IN YOUR NEW KIND OF NORMAL

Some of the struggles Mary the mother of Jesus encountered are similar to what many of us face today—escalating taxes resulting in financial challenges, political unrest, fears for the safety of family members, and conflicts within our houses of worship. The need to persevere in the face of personal, financial, church, and family challenges is as prevalent now as it was then. Certainly our standard of living is different from Mary's, but the emotional strain she experienced was not unlike today's stres-sors. There are moments in our lives when giving up on a person or a situation would be much easier than being in an indefinite period of waiting and not knowing what the end result will be. The physical and mental exhaustion of living "in the mean-time"—somewhere between an old and a new normal, creates the need for resolution. We ask questions. *How long will I wait for change? What other options do I have? Does God care about the anxiety this limbo is creating in my life?*

1. How do you typically deal with situations that involve waiting? Your answer could deal with something as simple

as sitting in the waiting room of a doctor's office or as important as waiting to find out whether you're going to be offered a job. What do you do "in the meantime" when there is an unwanted time period between your desire for action and the unknown result?

2. How does your response to waiting during this stage of your life differ from the way you waited as a teenager or as a young adult? What is the difference between waiting and perseverance, or do you think these words are synonyms? Do you value an answer more if you've had to wait for it for a long time? What are the benefits of waiting?

3. The Bible says that "suffering produces perseverance; perseverance, character; and character, hope. And hope does not disappoint us, because God has poured out his love into our hearts by the Holy Spirit, whom he has given us" (Rom. 5:3–5). When have you experienced the above progression in your life—a time when perseverance led to character and character led to hope? If you're not there yet, it's okay. This process doesn't usually happen overnight. Do you feel you are still struggling with the "waiting" part of perseverance, or have you moved into a time of character development, or are you now in a place where you have experienced hope that you can communicate to others? Why do you think suffering leads to perseverance?

4. When you desperately want relief from unrelenting reality, what do you usually do? Some of the ways I've tried to cope before I finally get to a biblical resolution are deny-

ing I have a problem, drowning myself in work, eating a big bag of potato chips or a large candy bar, casting blame on someone who should have "been there" to help prevent the problem, or going to the movies and escaping into someone else's life for a couple of numbing hours.

5. Do you agree or disagree with author Jan Frank: "Waiting in hope means that we rest our faith and expectation, not in what God will do for us, but on God who is our hope and expectation?"[4] If you agree, how hard is it for you to rest your hope in God without knowing if your situation will have a positive resolution in your lifetime?

6. Read the following Scripture passages:

- "Yet the LORD longs to be gracious to you; he rises to show you compassion. For the LORD is a God of justice. Blessed are all who wait for him!" (Isa. 30:18).

- "I wait for the LORD, my soul waits, and in his word I put my hope" (Ps. 130:5).

- "We wait for the blessed hope—the glorious appearing of our great God and Savior, Jesus Christ" (Titus 2:13).

- "I waited patiently for the LORD; and He inclined to me and heard my cry" (Ps. 40:1 NASB).

- "Wait for the LORD; be strong and let your heart take courage; yes, wait for the LORD" (Ps. 27:14 NASB).

Which of these verses best depicts where you are in your relationship with God if you are currently waiting on a specific answer to prayer or to a resolution of a crisis in your life? Write out the verse and then describe what gives you hope as you read the Scripture. If you don't feel hope yet, write out your questions to God, knowing He understands our deep pain in the middle of trying to persevere. Write the verse you selected on an index card and memorize it this week.

four
HOLDING ON TO HOPE

When I Feel Oppressed by My Disappointment and Sorrow . . . I CHOOSE GRATITUDE

THE SUPREME CHALLENGE TO ANYONE FACING
CATASTROPHIC LOSS INVOLVES FACING
THE DARKNESS OF THE LOSS ON THE ONE HAND,
AND LEARNING TO LIVE WITH RENEWED VITALITY
AND GRATITUDE ON THE OTHER . . .
LOSS CAN DIMINISH US,
BUT IT CAN ALSO EXPAND US . . .
LOSS CAN FUNCTION AS A
CATALYST TO TRANSFORM US.
—JERRY SITTSER

We were approaching the last weekend of May—the Memorial Day holiday. I had been invited to speak in Huntsville, Ontario, Canada, at a conference center situated on crystal-clear Mary Lake, located in the middle of an exquisite provincial forest. About four hundred women would be gathering at this Christian conference center for a celebratory weekend of crazy girlfriend antics, outdoor sports activities, delicious meals prepared by the resident chef, and a generous portion of spiritual inspiration and encouragement. That last item was my assignment—encouraging the participants with laughter, spiritual insight, and biblical truth.

As the time of our trip to Canada grew closer, I found myself anxious, agitated, and guarded. I began packing the suitcase, and a substantial heaviness came over me. This made no sense at all. I had spoken at this conference center numerous times in the past, and as a family we had reveled in the beauty of the area. I was looking forward to seeing many familiar faces at this event. People I care deeply about had made plans to attend. What was the source of this cloud of despair? Was I just overworked and tired? Or was something more troubling on my mind?

Gene had been irritable, and that was unusual for my optimistic, enthusiastic husband. He was the one who characteristically cheered *me* up and noticed when the looming shadows of depression were trying to overtake my mind and heart. He usually had an uncanny ability to recognize when I needed encouraging support, a change of scenery, or a ridiculous piece of trivia to break the dark mood. *What was going on with us?*

Early on Friday morning we arrived at the Orlando airport amid the usual hustle and bustle of families who were traveling home from Central Florida's many theme parks. Several children carried stuffed replicas of well-known Disney characters, and they were sporting miniature backpacks filled with other recently acquired souvenirs. Gene remained silent—uncharacteristically silent.

We moved through the security line at a snail's pace with few words passing between us. Gene was normally the first to make eye contact with a bleary-eyed child being dragged by a weary parent and ask, "Did you have fun on your vacation?" The child would smile and clutch a new action figure or stuffed animal and nod affirmatively. But not today.

Eventually we made our way to our assigned seats on the plane, and after takeoff, I guardedly asked, "Have I done something to tick you off? You are *never* this quiet, and I feel like there's a brick wall between us."

"No, it's not you," Gene calmly responded. "Haven't you learned by now that there are times when I need to grieve too?"

Instead of feeling criticized, I felt sad. Sad for all of my husband's losses. Sad for circumstances that couldn't be altered. Sad for lost hopes and dreams. Sad for the difficulty of facing familiar places that held happy family memories. Sad for an irreversible situation.

I saw tears brimming in Gene's eyes as he continued, "We're going to a place in Canada that was one of my favorite places to go with J.P.—and he won't be with me to go hiking in the forest and jumping from rock to rock in the pools at the foot of Ragged Falls. We won't be driving into Huntsville while you're speaking to reward ourselves with hamburgers and hot fudge sundaes after a day of challenging each other to hike a mile farther than we originally planned. He will *never* be with me again on a trip like this. I shouldn't have planned to come with you. I can't bear to face a place that holds such bittersweet memories."

I was quiet for the couple of minutes it took my mind to flash back to parts of what our "old normal" was as a family. During J.P.'s growing-up years, Gene worked in the insurance industry, and the company he worked for sent him on annual expense-paid trips to interesting destinations. These trips were part of his employer's incentive program, and frequently J.P. and I were able to join him at convention locations and tack on a few vacation days for family fun. My guys were thrill seekers, and they relished God's magnificent creation with gusto. As father and son, Gene and J.P. had hiked part of the Niagara Escarpment, explored the Smokies, and climbed Diamond Head in Hawaii. They had gone snorkeling in the U.S. Virgin Islands and swimming with the stingrays off the Cayman Islands. They even went snow camping in Canada in the dead of winter in four feet of snow at about fifteen degrees above zero. Jason was my husband's adventure-loving partner, and they challenged each other to excellence. In those moments, sitting beside my sad husband on the plane, I could hardly imagine how much Gene missed his son.

Suddenly, I felt compelled to be the "strong" one. With no forethought, I blurted out, "The fact that you don't *want* to go back to Canada is exactly why you *should* be coming on this trip. You have to force yourself to do what you love to do, whether or not J.P. is with you. Don't you see that the attitude of hopelessness you are allowing to wipe out your joy is exactly how the enemy intends to destroy you? He wants you to think you will never be happy again if things aren't like they once were. He wants you to be depressed when you climb mountains, hike through forests, and take on the adventure of the moment. He wants to gnaw at your emotions, make your memories of happier times better than they actually were, and make you believe you can never enjoy a sunset, an adventure, or a physical challenge again if your son isn't at your side. That's a lie from the pit of hell, Gene Kent! Get over it!"

I found myself shocked by the intensity of my own words. Gene was stunned momentarily, and then he began to smirk. His wry grin was followed by a low chuckle that quickly expanded into hearty laughter. "Well," he guffawed, "I guess you told *me*. Do you feel better?"

We laughed out loud, and Gene reached for my hand. He put his other arm around me and began to whisper a prayer close to my ear: "Lord, we are a mess! It's been more than six and a half years since our son was arrested, but it still feels like yesterday. Every time we think we are getting used to our new kind of normal, a memory, a trip to a familiar place, or a song on the radio reminds us that our lives will never be the same. Help us to quit taking our pain out on each other and help us to work together to be grateful for what we *do* have—which is a son who is still alive in an unlikely place.

"Thank You for our ministry to inmates and their families through Speak Up for Hope. Thank You for our precious family members and friends who support and love us and our son. Thank You that we have enough money to pay our bills after thinking we would never be out of debt again after J.P.'s arrest and trial. Thank You for giving us each other. You gave me a wife who loves me even when I'm distant and reluctant to communicate. Thank You for my beautiful, redheaded Carol Joy—who understands me and speaks up when I'm being a morbid recluse. Thank You for putting us together when we were teenagers and didn't even know we would be a good match for each other. Thank You for our son, who brings us great joy from the most surprising place—a maximum-security prison where he is a missionary in a facility that holds up to fifteen hundred inmates.

"Well, that's it for now, God. Help me on this trip to Canada. Enable me to take pleasure in the places I enjoyed going with my son without letting the enemy trick me into avoiding Your grand creation. I hate what I have lost, but I'm grateful You are giving me a heart tender to the needs of others. I'm grateful for a wife who puts up with my grumpiness and with my silent retreats into self-pity. Most of all, thank You for giving me a partner who understands and shares my pain. Amen."

Two hours later we landed in Toronto and made our way to northern Ontario. That evening was filled with the usual ministry routines—dinner with the meeting planner and other participants, setting up the book table, getting settled in our room, and speaking at the first session of the weekend-long event.

By Saturday afternoon, there was a break in the schedule. It was a picture-perfect day, with the sun falling to earth without the interruption of threatening clouds. Temperatures were warm, and Gene decided to make the trip back to Ragged Falls, thirty minutes away in one of the pristine Canadian provincial parks. It was a place where J.P. and his dad had formed a partnership in order to embark on a never-to-be-forgotten adventure as a father and son. Gene was worried that going alone to this special place would tarnish his valued memories of happier days. But he went anyway and later made this journal entry about his experience:

Sharp rock. Raging water. White foam blowing all over the place. Water sluicing off the ragged protrusions at unpredictable angles.

"Dad, let's go over there! Come on, Dad!" shouted my enthusiastic, adventure-loving, thirteen-year-old son.

I thought, No way can we make that distance. But we tried anyway, cheering each other on—and to the surprise of both of us, we made it. Rock to rock we moved in a forward direction with the swirling waters below, and we made it to the middle of the rushing stream.

Then we got stuck in the center of the river and could go no farther. There was a huge clear pool at the top of the falls, and it was tempting to swim there, but if we went off the edge, we knew we'd be mutilated. Not a good idea. Mom wouldn't like that. The sound of the reverberating falls was deafening. Piercing and thunderous. We could feel the call of adventure. It was distinct and wild, pulling at our bodies and imaginations. Maybe we'd fall in, and then what? Could we make it to safety?

"Son, take this step. Place your foot right here exactly where mine is. I'll move at the same time you move, and we'll make it together, one step at a time."

First, I'd find a path and he'd follow. Then he'd find a path and I'd follow. What an adventure! I can still hear the laughter and visualize the exploits of that day—a day I thought we would duplicate repeatedly in the future.

But everything has changed now. My only child has been sentenced to prison for the rest of his natural life. There will be no more hikes together. There will be no more rapids through which we can forge our escapade as a team—step by step. No more rocks to jump, and no more footsteps to walk in. He is my only son—my only child. Will he make it on this hideous journey in which his life is indefinitely on hold? Will I survive my own new kind of normal when my heart aches for former days when life was undisturbed with the challenges of today?

Ragged Falls was where it happened. Where the memories were made. Where we walked together. Where he grabbed for my hand. Where he trusted me to find a way out of the dead end. Where he yelled, "Help me!" which quickened this dad's heart.

But now we are faced with challenges much more intense than the raging waters of Ragged Falls. Will we allow the disappointment and sorrow of

Jason's life behind the razor wire to wipe out our hope, or will we still give thanks for what we do have? The choice is ours—individually and together. Will we give in to hopelessness, or will we acknowledge what we have to be grateful for? Will we build new memories in another place that will enable us to continue to partner in great adventures—far different from the physical exploits of our past but perhaps considerably more far-reaching?

Everything in me wants to just cave in to the grief I feel for my losses, which seem too great for a father's heart to bear. But I choose gratitude for what our father-and-son partnership can accomplish even in this unlikely place in our lives—with prison walls between our worlds.

The women's conference ended at noon on Sunday, and we once again found our seats on the plane in Toronto, buckled our seat belts, and heard the usual announcements from the flight attendant before our plane headed south. Gene put his arm around me, pulled me close, and whispered, "It was good for me to go on this trip. I found myself moving beyond the fear of facing the past and into a time of thanking God for the incredible memories I have made with J.P. We *are* a great team. We were buddies before his incarceration, and we still have a great relationship, in spite of the restrictions of prison. We have much to be grateful for."

THE POWER OF GRATITUDE AND PRAISE

Certain words go together—*gratitude, thankfulness, appreciation,* and *praise.*

There is a story in Acts 16 that reminds me of the power of praise and thanksgiving in the middle of a dark hour. Luke highlights the stories of three people who became believers through Paul's ministry in the city of Philippi. First, a wealthy business-woman named Lydia came to faith and was baptized. Following Lydia's conversion, God used Paul and Silas to transform the life of a demon-possessed slave girl who was being exploited for profit. The third person was the man entrusted with guarding Paul and Silas in jail after they were arrested in the middle of their mission trip.

> When the owners of the slave girl realized that their hope of making money was gone, they seized Paul and Silas and dragged them into the marketplace to face the authorities . . . The crowd joined in the attack against Paul and Silas, and the magistrates ordered them to be stripped and beaten. After they had been severely flogged, they were thrown into prison, and the jailer was commanded to guard them carefully. Upon receiving such orders, he put them in the inner cell and fastened their feet in the stocks.
>
> About midnight Paul and Silas were praying and singing hymns to God, and the other prisoners were listening to them. Suddenly there was such a violent earthquake that the foundations of the prison were shaken. At once all the prison doors flew open, and everybody's chains came loose. The jailer woke up, and when he saw the prison doors open, he drew his sword and was about to kill himself because he thought the prisoners had escaped. But Paul shouted, "Don't harm yourself! We are all here!" (Acts 16:19–28)

The jailer fell to his knees, trembling before Paul and Silas, and asked, "Sirs, what must I do to be saved?" (Acts 16:30) After they presented the gospel, the jailer responded, washed their wounds, brought Paul and Silas to his house, fed them a meal, and led his entire family to believe in God.

Bible scholars have described the kind of stocks Paul and Silas probably endured in jail. They were traditionally made of two boards joined with iron clamps. The captors left holes just big enough for the ankles. The prisoner's legs were placed across the lower board, and then the upper board was closed over them. Often both wrists and ankles were placed in stocks. Paul and Silas had committed no crime, but they were put in stocks designed for holding the most dangerous prisoners.[1] In spite of the discomfort and false arrest, they prayed and sang songs of praise.

The longer Jason is incarcerated, the more Gene and I understand the powerful principle demonstrated by the story of Paul and Silas. When we choose to focus on praise and gratitude, we get our focus off ourselves, off our son's shackles, off our hopelessness of ever seeing our son outside prison bars again, and off our personal disappointment. Showing gratitude has to do with appreciating benefits received and expressing that thankfulness to others. True gratitude evidences itself by bringing joy to others and alleviating their discomfort.

Paul and Silas demonstrated gratitude to God in the most unlikely circumstances. They prayed and sang while "the other prisoners were listening to them" (Acts 16:25). These men understood their mission: bringing the good news of the gospel to others, which in turn brought joy, freedom, faith, and comfort to everyone they encountered—even their jailer!

Our son was guilty of murder, but the principles we learn

from Paul and Silas have provided an extraordinary model for practicing gratitude in the middle of dismal circumstances. One of the most powerful survival tools we have is memorizing Scriptures that remind us to be thankful and to praise God. Here are a few of our favorites.

"Be thankful in all circumstances, for this is God's will for you who belong to Christ Jesus" (1 Thess. 5:18 NLT). We understood that the murder was not God's will for our son, but we needed to practice thankfulness to God regardless, or we would turn into bitter, angry people.

"Let us come to him with thanksgiving. Let us sing psalms of praise to him" (Ps. 95:2 NLT). We discovered early in our new normal how our mental and emotional responses changed as we verbalized our thanks to God aloud. We would walk hand in hand, eyes wide open, praying together along the St. Clair River in Michigan. We also purposefully played praise and worship music in our home. Even when we didn't feel like singing, we heard lyrics on CDs that were based on biblical truth. The healing words gradually captivated our hearts and renewed our thinking.

I will never forget this awful time,
    as I grieve over my loss.
Yet I still dare to hope
    when I remember this:
The faithful love of the LORD never ends!
    His mercies never cease.
Great is his faithfulness;
    his mercies begin afresh each morning.
I say to myself, "The LORD is my inheritance;

therefore, I will hope in him!"
The LORD is good to those who depend on him,
   to those who search for him.
So it is good to wait quietly
   for salvation from the LORD. (Lam. 3:20–26 NLT)

Gene and I know we will never forget the awful time of Jason's arrest, trial, and conviction—but we pray that we, too, will "dare to hope" when we remember the unfailing love of the Lord. When we are flat on our faces—broken, weeping, hurting, and questioning the effectiveness of our parenting, we know God keeps us from complete despair and destruction. That is when we practice being thankful for His mercies every morning by saying out loud what we are thankful for:

> *Lord, thank You that Jason did not receive the death penalty.*
> *Father, thank You for providing a buyer for our home*
>   *in Michigan so we could move closer to our son.*
> *Lord, we are grateful for the phone call from the father*
>   *of the deceased on Father's Day, telling us his son*
>   *knew You personally and is in heaven.*
> *Thank You that as we minister out of our brokenness,*
>   *people identify with our suffering and know that*
>   *we genuinely care about what they are experiencing.*

When I was visiting my son in prison recently, he told me that when depression tries to take him under a dark emotional cloud, he makes a list of what he has to be thankful for. Then he verbalizes those things to God in prayer. He usually experiences an instant change in his spirit as he focuses on being grateful. When he combines that action with looking around and seeing how he can assist a fellow inmate (with planning for a soon-coming release date, helping to connect that person with resources, or encouraging someone else with practical or biblical advice), he always has a positive change in his own attitude.

PRACTICING A MIND-SET OF GRATITUDE

I have often wondered if Mary, the mother of Jesus, continued to maintain her attitude of gratitude following her powerful song. Her profoundly tender response to an unexpected pregnancy—and by any measure, a potentially controversial pregnancy—expresses an unwavering faith, resolute trust, and deep thanks to God.

I wonder if she continued to choose gratitude during the bewildering and sorrowful moments when her family feared Jesus was crazy (Mark 3:20–21), at the Cross, or after the Ascension. I suspect she did, because Luke got his account of the details that unfolded in chapters 1 and 2 of his Gospel from somewhere, or from *someone*, and a portion of it appears to be information that nobody alive but Mary possessed. Based on historical research, we are told that Elizabeth, Zechariah, and Joseph all had probably died by the time of the Crucifixion. Several times Luke mentions that Mary treasured and pondered things in her heart. That means some of this information appears to have come from Mary, perhaps indirectly. If so, it seems likely that her song in Luke 1 remained the theme song of her life.

The attitude of Mary—so full of praise and the steadfast confidence that God is at work in ways we cannot see—gives me an example I long to follow. But choosing gratitude when current circumstances offer no hint that life will eventually turn out okay does not come naturally or easily.

Karen Beck, a gifted Bible teacher and mentor to many young women, e-mailed me on a day when I was having trouble praising God for my current circumstances. She wrote:

> . . . I had the benefit of being prostrate on the floor with a friend this year, weeping and entreating God for our children, when she took me to Acts 16 and had me read verses 25–26 out loud. She quizzed me about what the passage was saying, and like a good student, I said, "Yes, I know. I'm stuck and I need to practice praising God." But then she pointed out something I had never seen before. Paul and Silas's discipline of praying and praising not only broke their own chains, but it also broke the chains of every other inmate in the prison.
>
> This has been a profound truth for me to meditate on. When I give myself to acknowledging the mighty sovereign God of the universe in the midst of my great struggles and heartaches, I not only begin a process of release for my own heavy heart, but I also influence others who are in chains to lift their eyes heavenward, setting them free, as well.

I continued to read and was astonished to realize that Gene and I had somehow encouraged this insightful woman by choosing to act in faith even when we didn't *feel* God's power in our situation.

Carol, that's what you and Gene are doing as you continue to give yourselves to Him—saying with your lips and your lives that He is God and you are not . . . and you will continue to trust Him even though the outward evidences of what you desire are missing. Thank you for trusting Him to enable you to walk in your high, hard places. It is a fragrant aroma to our King like none other when we praise Him in the middle of unanswered prayer and unthinkable heartache. May His loving-kindness sustain you.

After reading Karen's note, I felt encouraged—and I praised God for letting me hear from someone who understood that the true intention of my heart was to honor Him, even in this unwanted situation and even when my feelings had trouble catching up.

The following story from Kathy reminds me that pain is pain. Whether your son is arrested for murder or your child gets caught in the chains of addiction, it's all pain—and choosing gratefulness is hard.

AN UNLIKELY PAIR—SORROW AND GRATITUDE

It was 2:30 a.m., and I had just gotten off the phone with a bartender. He called because he wanted my husband and me to know that our son was given a ride home and was in terrible shape. We live in a small community, and everyone knows everyone, so this man knew who we were. The caller told us it appeared that our son had been beaten up and was very drunk, and he feared our son might die.

We didn't go. Instead, I spent another sleepless night. This wasn't new to us. Every time the phone rang in the middle of the night, it was about our son. We had come to a point where we knew we couldn't help him. In fact, helping him seemed to hurt him. He was only twenty-eight years old. His wife had left him, and there wasn't anyone else to see if he was okay. I was holding on to hope and not really knowing what kept me believing. I was unable to pray. I found myself repeating Scripture verses I had memorized, but mostly, I waited.

We have two wonderful sons and love both of them greatly. We made mistakes in our parenting. Most parents do. I spent time reviewing the past several years in my mind, trying to figure out what went wrong.

This phone call was concerning our younger son, the same little blond boy who came home from kindergarten each day to play games with me. The one who liked to work in the garage and wanted me out there to watch him, because he was afraid to be alone. The one who begged to be baptized at age five because he knew he had Jesus in his heart. One night he cried over his sin when we took communion together as a family. He *loved* Jesus. But on his journey through life, he became addicted to drugs and alcohol. This addiction determined who he was and what he did. It was his god now, and he couldn't see Jesus anymore. His life was a mess, but I still believed that God would make up for "the years the locusts [had] eaten" (Joel 2:25).

He had almost died many times before the phone rang on this particular night. At age three, he sniffed gas and had to go the emergency room. He could have died then apart from God's intervention. He'd been in car accidents and later experimented with drugs of all kinds. He was always taking risks. We had done all we could to help him, including admitting him to treatment centers, trying different schools, and sending him to counseling sessions—but nothing seemed to make a difference. Now he was a husband and father, and even his family wasn't able to help him get the aid he needed to enter a recovery program.

This time he was on probation and had just been released from wearing an ankle bracelet that monitored him in his home instead of jail. I remember always being at peace when he was in jail—at least there he was safe.

He was found alive the next day and taken back to jail. His probation officer agreed that he needed help. He was placed in a Christian recovery center for one year. It was a miracle of mercy, and I was convinced this would be the time he would turn his life around. I dreamed about my prayers over the past several years being answered. My son would be free of any addictions and he'd be sharing his story of redemption.

Our dreams came true that year, and we were overjoyed to hear him share his story at church. He was even offered a job at the counseling center. But two weeks after he completed the program, he was drinking and using drugs again. The anguish and sorrow I felt at that time were incomprehensible. I honestly believed God had finally answered my prayers and rewarded my mother heart with a son who had changed his ways. But that was not the way this true story was playing out. *Why did God let this happen?*

Our life was never normal. I don't even know how to define that word. I always wanted everything to be okay, and now, facing the biggest letdown of my life, I realized our lives would never be normal. I had to find a different dream. Maybe I needed to quit dreaming at all. I always thought I could figure out what God *would* or *should* do. This latest disappointment changed me.

One day someone gave me a book called *Shattered Dreams*, by Larry Crabb. I promptly gave it to someone else. I didn't want to think that my dream for my son's life was shattered. Later a friend gave me her copy, and I thought perhaps I should read it, since it was placed in my hands twice.

The things God was teaching me were the opposite of what I had always believed. I had always thought that if I prayed hard and long enough, and with enough people joining me in prayer, God *had* to see things my way. I believed God didn't want me to experience pain. As I studied the life of Naomi, I understood a deep truth—Naomi was bitter after her sons died, and she was able to admit her honest feelings. She didn't try to cover them up by saying what people wanted to hear. Slowly, I began to learn that God wants to reveal Himself to me *in* my pain. I began to understand that God has to be enough—that He will help me *through* pain, and that He won't always deliver me *from* pain. I am still learning that it's in the pain that I can learn who He really is, that I can become like Him as I suffer.

I believe the reason I was still open to hearing what God had to say was the prayers of my grandmother. She was the mother of three alcoholics, and I know she endured many sleepless nights. But she continued to pray through all the generations. It was looking back, observing what God had done in the past, that continued to carry me through these days and the days that followed.

I am the keeper of my grandmother's Bible, and there is a

prayer in the front cover of that Bible that she prayed for all of her family. Even though she died decades earlier, I believe I was on that list and that God was still answering her prayer. It reads:

Dear Father God, It is through my faith in You that I can give my loved ones confidence. I would have them filled with Your love, life, joy, peace, and strength. Be with each one today, helping him with his problems. Be with me, also, my help in every need. Amen.

Then Grandma added Hebrews 13:5: "He will never leave you or forsake you." Then she wrote, "He never has!"

I believe it was this little prayer and the big faith of my grandmother that took me through all the pain in my life. I always had a thread of hope. I kept holding on because of her prayers. I wanted to quit, but somehow I never could. I had been prayed for long before all these hurts had descended on our family. It was the *history* that gave me hope! God was there in the past, He was here in my present, and He would be faithful in the future.

My grandmother left me a legacy of faith I didn't even know I had. I noticed she never asked God to take our problems away but asked Him to help us *through* them. I thought about all the times God had helped me through events that have broken my heart—and not just the events of my son's life. I have a broken heart, and that's normal for me. It may never be healed this side of heaven. That's okay. God uses my broken heart to keep me close to Him; without it, I might not need Him so much.

Looking back over the history of my life gives me confidence, just like my grandmother prayed. That's when the light came on for me. God was enough! He was then and He is now. Over the years I wanted to make things happen my way, to control my son's life and others' lives too. I've wanted to scream at God for mercy. I've been angry with Him for the way things are in my son's life and in mine. I've wanted to die. Yet somehow I haven't, and then I realize why I am grateful. There's always been joy in the sorrow and rainbows in the rain. The words from the hymn "O Love That Will Not Let Me Go" describe my life. God has given me so much during the hard times—always some incredible gift of joy.

My son is in a period of sobriety as I write, and I don't know what tomorrow will bring. Maybe this will be a new beginning for him. I hope so. But if it's not, I will live in my new normal each day, as God has ordained. He is more than enough; He is my life. He is bringing all my grandmother's loved ones to Himself, and I know someday we will be together again.

I'm grateful for my son and for all I have learned because of his life. I'm also grateful for my oldest son, that he and his family have helped me to hold on to hope, and I'm grateful for my five grandchildren whom I pray for every day.

I am deeply grateful for the legacy of a praying grandmother, for the joy in the pain, for the love of God who has always been there, for the people He has placed in my life, and for a husband who has walked with me through it all and has never given up. Most of all, I am grateful to God, who understands my pain and carries me through. His coming and dying are more than enough. I will choose gratitude, one day at a time.

WORSHIP BEHIND THE RAZOR WIRE

I, too, thank God for praying grandparents. Last weekend, my parents were visiting our son at the prison. My father is a former pastor, now retired, and we decided that since we couldn't attend church together, we would have our own service in the visitation room. My sister and brother-in-law, Bonnie and Ron, joined us, so we made up a congregation of six. Seated around the rectangular table with a Gideon Bible provided by the facility (since we are no longer allowed to take our own Bibles through security), Mom and Dad each read a Scripture and shared meaningful applications.

As I watched my eighty-three-year-old parents lead this prison-yard Sunday morning service, I reflected on some of the things that have changed since Jason's incarceration. Grandpa and Grandma's declining health is one of many unwanted changes. Mama now sat in a wheelchair, but her wrinkle lines crinkled as she spoke, and her eyes sparkled as she looked lovingly at my son. I could see her wince as she altered her position, and I knew that arthritis was making it challenging for her to move without pain. Dad leaned in and adjusted his hearing aid so he, too, could actively participate in the animated family conversation. After having a pacemaker surgically implanted only two weeks earlier, we prayed he wouldn't need nitroglycerin during the visit.

Mom and Dad had traveled from Michigan to see their first-born grandchild in prison. Each time they arrive at the airport, I wonder if it will be the last time they can make the trip. In spite of fragile health, their spirits are positive and encouraging. Dad always leaves the prison visits saying, "Jason is not only surviving; he's *thriving!*" My mother heart knows my son has downplayed the often horrific surroundings in which he lives to encourage his grandparents. I also know my father has been blessed as Jason shares what he is reading and as Dad picks up on how Jason is ministering to other inmates.

As our little worship service continued, Mother's face broke into a smile as she quoted from *The Living Bible*: "Don't worry about anything; instead, pray about everything; tell God your needs and don't forget to thank Him for His answers. If you do this you will know God's peace which is far more wonderful than the human mind can understand. His peace will keep your thoughts and your hearts quiet and at rest as you trust in Christ Jesus" (Phil. 4:6–7). I smiled, realizing those were the same verses she had *me* memorize as a child—only I needed them more now than I did decades earlier.

We took turns going around the table, sharing one thing we were thankful for and one request for prayer. When it was Jason's turn, he looked around at the faces of relatives who love him. In that moment, I think he realized these family members were not going away. They were there for him at his trial in Orlando, and they have written to him, visited him, sent magazines and books to him, and encouraged him consistently for the past seven years—and they will stand in the gap for him through prayer and active participation in his life for as long as they live. With a tremor in his voice, Jason said, "I'm thankful for family, and that you still care about me and love me."

Tears came to my eyes as my sister Bonnie quietly began to sing Fanny Crosby's great old hymn, the song we always sang at family reunions, usually around the dinner table while we lingered after a sumptuous meal. First it was a solo by Bonnie. "To God be the glory, great things He has done . . ." Then Grandma and Grandpa joined in, "Praise the Lord, praise the Lord, let the earth hear His voice! Praise the Lord, praise the Lord, let the people rejoice!" Finally, with tears streaming, I joined the rest of the family in musical gratitude to God. "O come to the Father through Jesus the Son, and give Him the glory—great things He hath done!" By the end we had added alto and tenor to our spontaneous choir.

I could almost see God smiling as He peered through heaven's glory to a prison visitation room on a Sunday morning and viewed His followers voicing their gratitude and praise through song. And I heard Him whisper in my ear, *Remember, you are not home yet. You are not alone. I see your son. I love him more than you do. Keep holding on to hope.*

GOD'S POWER IN YOUR
NEW KIND OF NORMAL

Many of us grew up in homes where we were taught to say please and thank you. During those years, we were learning to be polite. However, as life weaves its tapestry of good times and bad times, we face new decisions. The words *thank you* can be difficult to internalize when life seems unfair and it appears that God is not answering our prayers for a desired outcome. Sometimes it's easier to choose withdrawal and denial over active participation in life.

When it seems as though everyone around us is experiencing the abundance of God's blessings while our situation continues to spiral downward, expressions of thanksgiving and praise can disappear from our vocabulary. Sometimes, while deep in our own pain, it's hard to express joy to others who are experiencing God's blessing and abundance. We try to be happy for them, but inside we face a hard question: *I've tried hard to live my life as a Christian should, so why hasn't my life and my family situation turned out better?*

1. True gratitude consists of two elements: first, showing appreciation for benefits that are received, and second, bringing joy to others by supplying comfort to them during their time of need. Which of those two parts of this definition are you best at expressing? Is the one you didn't select hard for you to convey in a tangible way?

2. Review the story of Paul and Silas on page 83 or read it in Acts 16:19–28. What were the benefits these men experienced as a result of choosing to praise God and express gratitude for His goodness in the middle of their unjust incarceration? There are many kinds of prisons in our lives, and most are not behind bars. Have you ever been involved in a situation in which someone else's discipline of praying and praising not only broke his or her own chains but also liberated others in some way? Explain.

3. Most of us grew up in a home where our parents either often verbalized praise and gratitude or where they almost never voiced positive comments. On a scale of 1 to 10 (with 10 being the highest), how often did you hear praise or thanks from either or both of your parents? How did that affect you in your growing-up years? How has it influenced your current relationships?

4. This chapter includes two stories of godly grandparents—

our son, Jason's, grandparents, and Kathy's grandmother, who left a prayer in her Bible that encouraged Kathy through discouraging times with her son. Did you have a godly heritage, or were you brought up without a strong faith foundation? Whom have you looked to for encouragement, prayer, and advice during your new kind of normal?

5. Author Rebecca Barlow Jordan writes, "The blessing of gratitude is like a boomerang. When it flies out of a truly grateful heart, it hovers momentarily above the receiver, blessing its recipient, and then makes a 180-degree turn back into the life of the one who offered thanks."[2] Write this quote on an index card or on a sticky note and place it in a location where you spend a lot of time. Each time you experience that 180-degree blessing when you choose a grateful heart this week, record it as a reminder of the power of this important choice.

6. Think about your own new kind of normal. Make a list of ten things you have to be thankful for in the middle of an unexpected or an unwanted change in your life. Practice praying through that list, verbalizing your thanks to God for any benefit, however small, of your unforeseen circumstances.

five

MY HEARTACHE IS NONE OF YOUR BUSINESS!

When I Want to Keep My Feelings to Myself . . . I CHOOSE VULNERABILITY

> REVEALING OUR WEAKNESSES
> HELPS OTHERS FEEL CONNECTED TO US.
> FULLY UNDERSTANDING AND UNCONDITIONALLY
> LOVING US SHABBY HUMANS,
> JESUS SHOWS UP BEST IN OUR WEAKNESS.
> HE SHINES BRIGHTLY THROUGH THE CRACKS
> IN OUR FLAWED ARMOR.
> —BRENDA WAGGONER

I was visiting with conference participants in the lobby following a talk I gave about our painful journey through the aftermath of our son's arrest. One woman cautiously approached me, finding it difficult to make eye contact. Her stooped posture and somber demeanor told me she struggled with deep hurts.

Leaning toward me, she whispered, "My husband's been incarcerated for the past eighteen years—and nobody knows. He's getting out of prison in one month."

"Is he coming home to live with you?" I asked quietly, not wanting to reveal her secret to others who waited to speak with me.

"Yes, we're going to try to make a go of it," she said with a bit more energy in her voice. Then, almost miraculously, she stood tall, confident. With a smile, accompanied by good voice volume and unexpected boldness, she blurted out, "Today you've given me the courage to start telling my story! I am going to quit hiding in false shame and guilt, and I'm going to tell people what happened to our family. I'm going to give them hope, just like you gave me today." Following that quick announcement, she was gone. Her mission had begun.

Behind her stood three young women, holding hands. They appeared to be in their mid- to late twenties. One of them was the spokesperson for the group. "Thank you for telling us what happened to your family and for being honest about your son's crime and his incarceration. After you spoke and the event ended, we just sat in our seats, unable to get up. We're sisters. During our growing-up years, all three of us were repeatedly sexually abused by our father—and we've never told the secret."

The young woman's speech was labored, and her sisters held tightly wadded tissues in their free hands as they wiped fresh tears. She continued, "After you told the truth about your son's crime and how your family is trying to do something positive with this unwanted experience, we had a talk with each other. We've been hiding in our own denial, confusion, embarrassment, and shame—but if you can be brave and honest about your journey, we can too."

I could see these three lovely women—young moms who were now raising their own children—wanting life to be different and better for their offspring. The initiator of the conversation spoke up again. "We're going to get Christian counseling, and then we are going to share our own story in appropriate ways. Thank you for giving us the courage to be vulnerable and to begin taking positive steps in a forward direction."

By this time, all four of us were weeping. It was a day when God confirmed to me that in spite of great personal sorrow, He would scoop me up in my brokenness and use the fractured pieces of my life in a redemptive way.

In the past, prior to Jason's arrest and conviction, I had been a professional public speaker, holding my emotions together and carrying my own secrets close to my vest. I didn't want people to see me cry. I didn't want people to know I needed help. I didn't want people to know we were hurting financially. And I certainly didn't want others to feel sorry for me. That day I could almost hear God say, *Carol, I can use you best in your brokenness. When you are honest about your grief and the depth of your disappointment, without pretending everything is fine when it isn't, people listen to what you are saying.*

Once Gene and I started being vulnerable about what had happened to us by talking about our experience with Jason, we were stunned by how quickly other people started telling us about their own distressing circumstances. Whenever we opened our e-mail inbox or our postal mailbox, we found story after story from people who had cracked open their hearts to reveal the sometimes frightening, often devastating truth of their own lives.

I have read your book *When I Lay My Isaac Down* twice, and every day I go back over the parts I have highlighted. My twenty-six-year-old son was an honor roll student and a football player throughout high school. He received an academic scholarship for college, but three years ago he was diagnosed with schizophrenia. He is now living in a group home for the mentally ill. He is on heavy medication, which has helped with the hallucinations, but he still has delusions and paranoia. He is nothing like the son I raised. It is as if that child died, and the mourning is relentless because his body is still here . . . I pray one day that I, too, can adjust to this new kind of normal and speak openly about our journey.

My husband, a convicted sex offender, is incarcerated in a state prison. He was in ministry, and our journey has been crushing. We have gone through bankruptcy, the loss of our home, and financial ruin. I was laid off from my job and I have three children to support. Due to the nature of my husband's crime, I have lost many friends. As time goes by, people go on with their lives and forget we are hurting and need emotional support. Many family members and some of my husband's former staff snub me because of what my husband did. We live in a small town and reporters showed up on my doorstep. They took a picture of our house that appeared on the local television news. I long to have a support group where I can be "real" with people who understand this horrible experience. Due to the nature of my husband's crime, talking openly about our experience is challenging, to say the least. I feel so alone.

I am a forty-two-year-old single mom. I was incarcerated in Connecticut's maximum-security prison for twelve months on a charge of larceny. I embezzled money from a previous employer to fund my gambling addiction. I have a twelve-year-old son, and I am now divorced due to my addiction. I cannot fathom what you have been through and how you can stand before so many people and pour out your heart. As I listened and cried, it brought back a lot of pain for me. I can't imagine ever facing a life sentence. It was heart-wrenching for my son and my family to go through this experience with me. But as I faced the truth of my choices and shared honestly with others, I was overwhelmed by the unconditional love and support of my church family.

Everything you wrote about in your book about the prison experience is true. I have been so frustrated with the whole system! The money they are making off of inmates' families through exorbitant phone charges and fees deducted every time money is deposited in an inmate's account really upsets me. When our son's grandmother sends a $20 money order to our son's "commissary fund" so he can purchase deodorant and stamps, the system deducts a $2 deposit fee. Thank you for swallowing your pride and being vulnerable about the ugly, hidden side of the prison system that nobody talks about.

When Jason was first arrested, it was a gigantic ordeal to talk with relatives and close friends about what had happened. At that time, we were grieving so much we could hardly put words to our feelings. Two and a half years later, the trial, conviction, and sentencing were over—and we had to make a choice: Would we hide from people, public platforms, and potential embarrassment, or would we honestly face the world with the truth of our experience?

THE UNWANTED INTERVIEW

The *Dateline NBC* producer didn't smile. She met with us over coffee in Orlando and told us that the popular TV news-magazine was going to feature the story of Jason's trial. They were not asking us if they could have permission to do so. Our only choice in the matter was in regard to how the story might be told. Would we agree to be interviewed in our hometown, or would the program's producer simply use snippets of our story from the trial that had been videotaped by *Court TV*? She strongly suggested the program would appear less biased if we told our side of the story. We knew the viewing audience would be more than ten million people. After seeking wise counsel, we finally agreed. We were not given the questions ahead of time and didn't know if the interview would be structured as an attack on our parenting, on our son, and on our character.

Gene and I did not want to be interviewed in our home. It felt much too invasive to consider having strangers from NBC set up their hot lights and do their interview in the place that held significant memories of J.P. before all the horror began. So the *Dateline* handlers arranged to do the interview at a restaurant about twenty minutes from our home. On the appointed morning, Gene and I dressed, speaking very little. I struggled internally. *Hadn't we suffered enough already? Hadn't we testified in front of unwanted, glaring cameras we couldn't keep out of the courtroom? Were Gene and I on trial too? Why do we have to submit to this voyeuristic interrogation that will be aired during prime time on national television?*

When we arrived at the River Crab Restaurant along the St. Clair River, my stomach was doing cartwheels. I glanced down a row of booths and remembered the lobster dinner we had enjoyed with J.P. on the night we celebrated his appointment to the U.S. Naval Academy. It was a milestone in his life—and one of our happiest memories before he left for Annapolis. Now this same place had been turned into an interrogation room. I had not felt this vulnerable since the last day of Jason's trial.

Rob Stafford was the assigned interviewer. He asked hard, invasive questions, but he was doing his job. I kept tissues close by because my emotions were still raw. The bottom line was that no one could make sense out of what triggered a young man with an impeccable record and a good upbringing to shoot and kill another human being. We were as honest as we could be and revealed as much as possible about the joy it had been to raise Jason Kent and about the shocking events that had taken place on the day of the murder.

When the interview wrapped up, we had no idea how our responses would be edited into the final program. It was six months from the time of the interview until the program aired. When it finally did, we realized the producer had tried to be as fair to all parties as possible, and we experienced a remarkable outpouring of love and support from friends, as well as from people who had never heard of us before. Flowers were delivered to our home, calls came from faraway ministry acquaintances who had not heard about Jason's arrest, and written prayers and blessings arrived in the mail.

One of the most powerful letters from a viewer was from a psychologist who had worked with victims of sexual and emotional abuse for many years. She was appalled that a sexual abuse expert was not put on the stand following Jason's wife's testimony at his trial. It was too late to change a jury conviction for first-degree murder, but we were stunned by how much personal encouragement we received simply because we had opened up about the trial, our family, our pain, and our broken dreams.

WHAT IS VULNERABILITY?

The root word for *vulnerability* comes from a Latin verb that means "to wound," and it is related to another Latin verb form that means "to pluck." How appropriate! Being vulnerable about the most personal and painful details of our lives definitely produced a wounding of our souls, and we felt as though the media was "plucking" sound bites out of us for their own financial gain.

The dictionary defines *vulnerability* as "capable of being physically wounded" and "open to attack or damage."[1] We certainly understood. Our physical wound was inflicted internally due to extreme stress, but we also knew this television program and other newspaper and magazine articles could make us wide open to attack and potential damage due to rumors and conjecture. What I found most interesting in the definition is that *vulnerability* also means "liable to increased penalties, but entitled to increased bonuses after winning a game in contract bridge."[2] We certainly weren't playing bridge, but because of our willingness to be vulnerable, we were beginning to receive "increased bonuses" alongside our unwanted liability to "increased penalties."

The alternative to vulnerability is to conceal our secrets, hide our hurts, run from a community of caring people, lock up our feelings, and live in the dark shadows of loneliness. It's possible to be held in bondage by our deepest secrets, always wondering when "the day of revelation" will be sprung on us. The anxiety we experience can deplete energy, cause illness, stifle creativity, devastate relationships, and trigger addictions. A heart tormented by fear of the what-ifs begins to die slowly as it falls prey to hopelessness, a sense of unfairness, a loss of joy, and a belief that people are not to be trusted. Gene and I both knew that's not how we wanted to live. We had another choice to make.

MARY'S CHOICE

The first thing Mary did after she learned she was pregnant (or maybe about to be pregnant) was travel to her cousin Elizabeth's home. She spent three months there (Luke 1:39–45, 56). It was common in those days for a pregnant woman to go to a relative's home for some months of solitude for the health of mother and baby.

In Mary's case, we can imagine she needed some emotional support, as she was pregnant and betrothed. Her parents would have been furious about her pregnancy, and she had no idea what Joseph might do. He could have prosecuted her for adultery under the laws of the day. And until she got to Elizabeth's home, she may have wondered if she would be welcome there. Would Elizabeth believe the farfetched story of an angel predicting a virgin birth?

Let's read what happened:

A few days later Mary hurried to the hill country of Judea, to the town where Zechariah lived. She entered the house and greeted Elizabeth. At the sound of Mary's greeting, Elizabeth's child leaped within her, and Elizabeth was filled with the Holy Spirit.

Elizabeth gave a glad cry and exclaimed to Mary, "God has blessed you above all other women, and your child is blessed. Why am I so honored, that the mother of my Lord should visit me? When I heard your greeting, the baby in my womb jumped for joy. You are blessed because you believed that the Lord would do what he said." (Luke 1:39–45 NLT)

What a welcome greeting that was! Mary didn't have to wait long to know Elizabeth was receiving her with open arms and a glad heart. I believe God had already softened the heart of Elizabeth due to her own pregnancy. Scripture records that Zechariah was a priest, and Elizabeth was the daughter of a family of priests of the house of Aaron. Husband and wife were advanced in age and had been childless for many years. The Bible records that they were upright in God's sight and obeyed His commandments. God chose to bless them in their old age with a baby, John the Baptist, who would become an evangelist and proclaim the coming ministry of Jesus, the Messiah.[3]

Why do I think these two women were vulnerable with each other about their dreams, fears, physical changes due to pregnancy, and their faith? Because they spent a lot of time together! We read, "Mary stayed with Elizabeth about three months and then went back to her own home" (Luke 1:56 NLT). I wonder if Elizabeth coached Mary through the nausea of her early pregnancy. They no doubt talked about what a hero Joseph was. Ralph Gower gives us a glimpse into Joseph's character in *The New Manners and Customs of Bible Times:*

> Joseph did not want to expose her publicly, because as a supposed adulteress, Mary would have been stoned to death. It must have taken a great deal of love for Mary and a great deal of trust in God speaking through his dream that enabled Joseph to marry her. Maybe this is a reflection of the character God looked for in the man who was to bring up Jesus.[4]

Can you imagine all that these female cousins must have talked about? As the oldest of five sisters in my family, I know we share at a vulnerable heart level when we spend significant amounts of time together. Mary and Elizabeth were both pregnant under unusual circumstances—for Mary, an immaculate conception, and for Elizabeth, a late-life pregnancy. They no doubt discussed their changing bodies, their thoughts on child rearing, their personal challenges due to unique circumstances, and their extraordinary excitement about the coming birth of the Messiah! Both of these women would have identified with the meaning of vulnerability—"liable to increased penalties, but entitled to increased bonuses." What a joy (and burden) it must have been to be chosen by God to birth Jesus and John the Baptist.

MY BRAVE HUSBAND

Gene has an emotional and spiritual strength admired by many, including me. He is almost always even-tempered and calm in the face of the storm. He wants to appear as if he has thought of everything and has tried all the solutions. His motto is, if he can't handle it or do it, it can't be done. So for him to just speak honestly about what's going on in his life—and that he can't handle it or doesn't understand it or doesn't like it one bit!—has been a big step to take. He recently wrote down some of his thoughts about this uncomfortable choice.

The most difficult people I find to be transparent with are men. We are supposed to have it all together. We are supposed to take care of our families. We are supposed to raise our children "right." We are supposed to be able to cope with any problem that comes our way. Now, it's fairly easy to be open around women, because they already know how insecure men are. The Lord gave them such good insight and understanding. Men, on the other hand, are always talking about doing stuff, fixing stuff, and helping their kids with stuff.

My problem is too big for me to fix. I've tried and I've failed. What are the guys going to think? He's a loser. He can't take care of his own family. He can't straighten out his own son. *I know all these thoughts are wrong, but the society we live in was forged by "rugged individualists" who could solve their own problems.*

Our family's experience over the past several years has led me to discover that I need help. And I need it from anyone who is willing to help me. I have found by telling our story that people come out of the crowd to tell me their story and to share how they cope. I'm not telling a great success story. I'm telling of a failure. By being transparent about it, I connect with other men who have felt threatened by the "capable male syndrome" and how they don't measure up. Now they've met another man who doesn't measure up, and he still is normal, loves God, trusts God, and has hope for the future.

They begin to see that they can have hope too! As I share how I don't have it all together, they find the freedom to not have it all together either.

There is an unexpected and powerful camaraderie in our common pain. We may not have the same circumstances, but we do have the same pain, the same insecurity with handling life, and the same fear of losing everything. But God loves us anyway. He went through the turmoil of losing His own Son and came out the other side without changing. He will be with us in the midst of our mess and not call us losers or failures. He has our back and He has our front. The storm may be raging, the people may be talking, the circumstances may appear grim; but He goes through it with us and, thus, gives us hope.

MY BRAVE FRIEND

Lynn D. Morrissey is a gifted writer and a woman of influence. As our friendship has developed, I've observed some characteristics about Lynn that have increased my respect for this remarkable woman. She is intelligent, compassionate, and encouraging. Most of all, she is a person of truth, who isn't afraid of facing what people think if her vulnerability can help even one other person to make the right choice. She demonstrates what Max Lucado once said: "We hide. He seeks. We bring sin. He brings a sacrifice. We try fig leaves. He brings the robe of righteousness."[5] Here, in her own words, is her story of redemption.

❧

It was the last night of our women's Bible study on emotional healing, and as the facilitator, I was eager to hear women share about how God had used His Word to heal their wounds. While driving to church, I prayed, "Dear Lord, I know it will be extremely painful for many of these women to reveal their stories, but grant them courage and give them grace. As they name their pain and share their healing, other women will receive hope—perhaps for the first time."

After a wonderful evening of heartfelt sharing, I was about to close in prayer when a middle-aged woman timidly raised her hand. Jenny had been quiet while other women bared their souls, and I could tell she had something significant to say.

After several halting and tearful attempts to speak, words of anguish spilled from her trembling lips: "Years ago, I had an affair with a married man and became pregnant. I couldn't bear for my church family to know the truth, so I had an abortion. During this Bible study we've done together, I have confessed my sin to God. Now I need to confess it to you." For what seemed like an eternity, silence descended like a shroud. No one moved. No one spoke.

How I admired Jenny's courage and appreciated her vulnerability. I understood that sometimes when Christians rightly condemn the sin of abortion, they forget that women who commit this sin are in dire need of God's healing and forgiveness. When believers speak harshly about the sin, they often unwittingly compound the pain of women who suffer secretly.

Hadn't one of my friends at church just spoken to me about "such women" last week? "Lynn, how can women do that?" Marjorie asked. "How can they murder their own children? They must be the coldest, most callous creatures imaginable. They are detestable!" Little did Marjorie know that she was speaking directly to one of those heartless, loathsome creatures!

When I was a brand-new Christian, I had an abortion. I had never wanted to be a mother and had a morbid fear of dying in childbirth. When I learned I was pregnant, I felt trapped. I had not yet made Christian friends to whom I could unburden my fear. I had bought the "blob-of-tissue" deception and didn't believe I would be doing anything wrong. I asked my pastor for counsel, and he corroborated the lie. Not once did he show me the truth about conception in Scripture. Instead, he handed me the business card of his friend who was the director of a local abortion clinic!

After the procedure, on a jewel-blue summer's day, I can honestly say that I felt nothing—no remorse, no regret. I simply felt relief. In fact, I felt free. Yet this freedom eventually gave way to relentless guilt. God began to pierce my heart's armor with testimonies of post-abortive women I'd hear on the radio. And then one day, I read verses in Psalm 139 with new eyes and deepening horror: "For you created my inmost being; you knit me together in my mother's womb . . . your eyes saw my unformed body. All the days ordained for me were written in your book before one of them came to be."

These words of wonder and beauty were like daggers piercing my heart, mind, and soul. *Oh God!* I cried. *You planned us intricately. You meant for all babies to be born!* I was finally being honest with myself. I confessed my sin to God.

And for the next eighteen interminable years, I confessed my sin over and over and over again. I knew intellectually that God had forgiven me, but I didn't know it experientially. Surely I must assuage my guilt by doing something, *anything,* to atone for my child's death. I couldn't bring back the daughter I'd named Shannon, but I could pay for what I'd done to her. I did service projects. I led Bible studies. I worked with children. Absolutely nothing cauterized the wound in my soul.

As I continued to read articles about abortion, I came to a realization: *Oh, Lord, that's it!* I reasoned. *I need to speak out and educate people about this life-and-death issue. The only way to make up for Shannon's death is to help preserve life.* Yet each time I tried to write an anonymous article or volunteer at a pregnancy center, the door was blocked. Another pastor for whom I worked at the time wouldn't even publish a short antiabortion article I'd written for the church newsletter. "Lynn," he said, "this is a powerful piece against abortion, but I'm afraid that post-abortive women will feel condemned."

And no wonder . . . my own words were really condemning myself. Later that night, I cried out to God: *How can you ever forgive me for murdering my own baby—a baby with a name, a life, a soul, a destiny? How can I ever forgive myself?* In His mercy, God would soon answer those questions and grant me miraculous healing on a sunny Sunday at the edge of the ocean.

I had been participating in a secular journaling retreat. On the last day, participants gathered on the beach, where the facilitator asked us to write about a self-inflicted wound from which we had never healed. She asked, "What does grace feel like? Are you ready to forgive yourself?" She recited a little verse: "I want to go where the waters overflow. I'm ready to let them wash over me. If it's love flowing freely, I'm ready. If the waters can redeem me, I'm ready."

I immediately thought of my abortion—the mortal wound I'd inflicted on my child, the agonizing wound I'd inflicted on myself, the wound that had festered and oozed and contaminated my heart with self-loathing and guilt for so many years. Was I ready to receive God's grace? Oh, how I wanted to! Was I finally ready to forgive myself? I knew I had to. After all, Jesus had paid for all my sins or none.

As I looked out over the watery expanse, I lifted my pen and spilled my soul into my journal:

Oh, God! Your grace is fluid, flowing, flooding, unleashed, unlimited, unmeasured, undeserved—a gift bestowed without merit, without cost to me, free*—a ceilingless sky, a relentless riot of rain, a shoreless, bottomless ocean, there for the taking by the teaspoonful, cupful, bucketful, basinful, whatever amount for whatever need. And, with the taking, no diminishing supply—unending, unfathomable.*

For almost twenty years since the abortion, I've sandbagged the flow of Your grace and lay dying in the sand—parched and shriveled like snakeskin, thick-tongued, cotton-eyed, unable to see or speak or receive forgiveness, unable to walk to the water to plunge my festering heart into Your ocean's depths for cleansing release. I'm Bethesda Pool's paralytic— immobile—waiting for You to stir the waters, lift me up, and put me in to baptize my wounds in the sea of Your grace, to bury my sin in the depths of the ocean. With Your help, I would be satisfied now to swallow even the tiniest raindrop of grace. I'm dying of thirst—thirst for Your love, thirst for Your pardon.

Oh, Lord, I'm ready. I come to the water. Your love flows freely. I'm ready to receive it. Your living waters can redeem me. I'm ready—ready to let Your oceans of mercy, oceans of love, wash over me. I receive now the fullness of the forgiveness You gave me when You opened wide your arms on Calvary's cross—when You died for my sin of abortion. Lord, I'm ready. I'm ready.[6]

When we were finished writing, the facilitator asked us to read our entries out loud to the group. How could I possibly do that? Because of earlier conversations we'd had, I knew that the majority of my fellow participants championed women's so-called right to abortion. I had firmly stood my ground against it, claiming that abortion always means taking an innocent life. But now I would be admitting that I, myself, had murdered my own child. These people would brand me a Christian hypocrite, and I would bring shame upon the name of Christ. Yet my heart was so filled with God's grace, it simply had to overflow.

With great fear and faltering, through tears, I read my prayers and for the first time unveiled my secret sin. The impact my words had on my listeners is indelibly etched in my mind, their kindness forever written on my heart. One by one, each participant came forward, tears brimming in their eyes as they cradled me in compassion and love. They told me that they would never think of abortion in the same way again. I believe that if God had not given me the courage to share my pain in a public way, I would never have *felt* forgiven in the way I finally did. It is difficult to describe the fathomless freedom I experienced, the complete release, the weightlessness in my chest, the peace opening up in my heart like a fluttering of wings.

Now, eight years later, God had put *me* in the position of group facilitator, and Jenny had just unveiled her own long-held secret. Suddenly I felt petrified to reveal my past to my own Bible study companions. My mind reeled: *How will our pastor react when he finds out? Will he ask me to step down from leadership? What will these women think? They'll think I'm a horrible hypocrite; they'll hate me! How can I disappoint them?* Yet I knew I couldn't let Jenny stand alone. I needed to make a decision. *Oh God, please help me. Help Jenny,* I begged silently. Putting my arm around her, through my tears, I shared the truth about my own abortion.

The women were silent no longer. Each one wept. Each one rose from her chair. Each one gently descended upon Jenny and me like a garment of grace in the warm embrace of acceptance and love.

And then the most incredible thing happened: these same women began to lance deeper wounds about which they had not spoken earlier, exposing not only their pain but their guilt. Jillian had had an affair for many years with a married man and had aborted three children. Nancy, too, had been adulterous. Ginger grieved that she had been a terrible mother. Anna repented over her shoplifting days.

On and on, women lifted up their confessions to God as they laid down their burdens of fear, self-protection, self-hatred, and pride. And as they did, something remarkable happened to *me.* Seeing firsthand the healing power of corporate confession, I knew that God was calling me to start sharing openly in Christian circles about my abortion.

Public confession is sometimes necessary for full healing and restoration. In his book *Your God Is Too Safe,* Mark Buchanan writes:

Confession is when we quit all the deal making, the sidestepping, the mask wearing, the pretense and preening, and we get bone-deep honest before God: I am the man! . . . Everyone can, I think, agree with that definition of confession. But now here's a sub-clause: *In order to present our real selves to God, we need to be honest with ourselves about ourselves, and honest about ourselves to at least one other trusted and godly person* . . . I am not saying that if you don't confess to another person, God doesn't cleanse you from sin. I am saying, though, that we often do not *experience* the reality of God's cleansing apart from an honest confession to another person.[7]

If I could go back, I would never have aborted baby Shannon. There is nothing normal about abortion. It goes against nature and a mother's deepest instinct to protect her child. My sin destroyed her life, and it nearly destroyed mine. If I could do it again, I would give my life for hers, but I can't.

Yet I can live a "new normal." I am truly a new woman in Christ. Yes, He made me a "new creation" when He saved me, but I finally know what it means to live in the newness and freedom of forgiveness. My new normal means being still scarred by sin but not devastated by it. My new normal is not being afraid to share about the pain in my past, because God has given me peace in my present. When I laid my Isaac down, God gave me the privilege of helping to lift women up. And as they lay their Isaacs down, God is lifting them to a "new normal" too. There is nothing more normal than for the God of mercy and grace to redeem and restore broken lives. It's not only normal—it's *amazing*![8]

THE COST AND THE CAUTION

The "wounds" of being vulnerable mean some people will turn their backs on us, judge us, and criticize us in front of others. The cost can be high. However, the "healing" of being vulnerable means we no longer live in fear of having our secrets revealed. I am not advocating starting every conversation with our worst struggles. There are times and places when God leads us to speak up, but we need to be aware of when it is appropriate and whom it will impact. In the process of responding to the divine nudge of His voice, we discover amazing freedom and contagious joy. Our openness, when fitting, makes us a magnet for the people around us who are longing for just one person in their lives to be "real," to listen to their story without raising an eyebrow, to let them weep without providing advice. I know because I am walking this road. And it's worth the risk.

GOD'S POWER IN YOUR
NEW KIND OF NORMAL

Being vulnerable with other people can feel frightening and invasive. We find ourselves watching the reactions of the person who is listening to our story; we wonder if his or her facial expression is indicating disapproval, condemnation, pity, understanding, sympathy, or genuine concern. When we choose disclosure in an appropriate setting with people we trust, the surprising result is that people feel connected to us. Instead of being competitors who are trying to impress each other with how perfect we are, we become fellow strugglers who are attempting to live out our faith in an authentic way. Our carefully constructed facade melts away and is replaced with the genuine version of ourselves. The first step—being honest with even one person about the imperfect choices or situations of our lives—is the most challenging. Fear taunts, *People will reject you and make you feel like a flawed person.* Faith says, *Take the risk. Be real. Allow God to use the broken places of your past to give hope to someone else.*

1. How do you define the word *vulnerable?* Is it easier for you to be open with people you aren't likely to see again or with people who know you personally? Some people are afraid of being vulnerable because someone they trusted held their secret too loosely or betrayed them. Others want to hide the difficult and challenging parts of their lives in a dark closet, hoping the information will never surface. Others practice self-revelation naturally, even indiscriminately. Which of these ways of coping with crisis best describes you?

2. What are the benefits and the liabilities of being vulnerable? When do you think being vulnerable is inappropriate? When is it helpful?

3. The definition of the word *vulnerable* is: (a) capable of being physically or emotionally wounded, (b) open to attack or damage, and (c) liable to increased penalties but entitled to increased bonuses.[9] Pick one of the definitions and think about a personal experience when you were vulnerable. When you have risked being vulnerable with someone, has it been a positive or a negative experience? What were the benefits? Was your decision to be vulnerable worth the risk you took to be open and authentic? If you are going through these questions with someone else or with a small group, share your responses aloud.

4. Author Brenda Waggoner says, "Revealing our weaknesses helps others feel connected to us."[10] Do you agree or disagree with that statement? Why?

5. Read the following verses:

- "All my longings lie open before you, O Lord; my sighing is not hidden from you" (Ps. 38:9).

- "Nothing in all creation is hidden from God. Everything is naked and exposed before his eyes, and he is the one to whom we are accountable" (Heb. 4:13 NLT).

- "God, investigate my life; get all the facts firsthand. I'm an open book to you; even from a distance, you know what I'm thinking" (Psalm 139:1–2 MSG).

These verses indicate that God knows our thoughts and the longings of our hearts. Yet sometimes it's hard to pray with authenticity. On a scale of 1 to 10 (with 10 being the highest), how vulnerable are you when you talk to God? Do you feel comfortable telling Him you are hurt or angry or frustrated? Why or why not?

6. Read Lynn Morrissey's powerful prayer on p 126. How did she describe God's grace? How did she portray her need? What was the result of her prayer? Think of a time when you were vulnerable with God about a wrong choice you made or a hurt you faced. How did He respond to you? Did you feel comforted? Confused? Forgiven? Ashamed? Reassured? Being vulnerable is hard. At this stage in your journey, what do you need to be honest about with God? Consider writing out your response in the form of a heartfelt prayer or sharing it in detail with someone you can trust.

six

LOSS UPON LOSS

When Nothing Goes According to My Plan . . . I CHOOSE RELINQUISHMENT

LIVING WITH A MIRACLE MEANS FAR MORE
THAN EXPERIENCING ITS CONCEPTION.
IT MEANS RESTING IN GOD'S PROMISE AND POWER
EVEN WHEN IT SEEMS THE MIRACLE
ISN'T GOING TO BE BORN.
—JACK HAYFORD

The e-mail was unexpected. It came from an influential person in a governmental position in the state of Florida. A friend had suggested he get in contact with us. I immediately thought it was because of Jason—perhaps this person would have some idea about what we should do next as advocates for our son. But that wasn't the case. He had heard I did communications training seminars and was interested in knowing how to speak more effectively. I responded by saying that two of my books might be helpful: *Speak Up with Confidence* (because it gives the how-tos of speaking) and *When I Lay My Isaac Down* (as an example of putting a message together based on your own faith story). I let him know I would be happy to send the books as a gift if an address could be provided. He immediately said he would get them on his own.

Eight days later, another e-mail arrived. He had read the book on our journey with our son—from Jason's arrest to his conviction and sentencing—and his latest note said: "I feel strongly your son should make application for his case to be heard in front of the Florida Clemency Board in December of 2006, before Governor Jeb Bush leaves office due to term limits." A burst of hope exploded in my heart. *Somebody who works in the Florida government believes there is a chance, even a small chance, that the Clemency Board would believe Jason P. Kent did not need to be locked up for the rest of his life.*

My mind spun as I recalled the many other people we had met through the years, in and out of Florida governmental circles, who were able to connect us to people of influence who could provide advice and tangible help. Gene and I would look at each other and say, "Now, *that* was a divine appointment!" It had happened again and again—and now again. I wondered if perseverance had finally paid off and God was at work on a new kind of miracle.

I replied, "This is so exciting. Jason has only been incarcerated for six and a half years, and we thought it was probably too early to begin the clemency process."

The response was encouraging: "Many people don't understand that clemency doesn't always mean instant release of an inmate. The clemency process can result in a commutation of sentence, which means setting an end-of-sentence date. In your son's case, with a conviction of first-degree murder, you would definitely not be looking at instant release. The most you could hope for would be to receive an eventual end-of-sentence date."

I had almost forgotten what hope felt like, so I was exuberant. Even if Jason's sentence was commuted to twenty to twenty-five years, he would still walk in freedom in his lifetime since he committed the crime when he was twenty-five-years old.

Gene and I had lots of questions, and we began to form a plan of action. Several specific steps had to be taken in less than four months.

1. Petitions needed to be signed by people who believe Jason will not be a threat to society if he is ever released. These petitions could be from anywhere in the country, and they needed to ask the governor to fast-track Jason's case so it could be heard at the clemency hearing in December 2006.

2. We also needed to locate at least three people of influence, particularly people in government, who would write a personal letter to Governor Bush and to the clemency board asking for the fast-tracking of Jason's case.

3. Certified paperwork on his case from the clerk of the circuit and county courts had to be filed with Jason's application for clemency. Little did we know this seemingly small step would be very challenging due to how slowly paperwork is duplicated and mailed from many government offices.

4. Letters of support for Jason needed to be collected for the clemency board from people who knew Jason before

and/or after his incarceration. These letters needed to voice confidence in Jason's character and assurance that our son had a strong network of family and friends who would assist him upon release. Most of all, the letters needed to assure the clemency board that he would not be a threat to society if granted freedom at some point in the future.

The assignment ahead of us was daunting but not impossible. The first thing we did was make a list of prayer needs, including specific people we were praying for in this process. As the mother of Jason Kent, a concern that loomed like a sinister shadow was getting Jason's hopes up once again, knowing there was an enormous likelihood that our brand-new "house of hope" would topple into ruins.

THE MARATHON BEGINS

Suddenly, in the middle of multiple out-of-state ministry trips, every spare minute of our at-home time was devoted to our new dream of getting Jason's case heard at the December clemency hearing. Our "Stretcher Bearers," the extraordinary group of family members and friends who received monthly updates on how to pray for our family and how to help meet our tangible needs prior to the trial, had waited a long time for an update, and many people had been contacting us to ask what they could do to help Jason's case.[1] It had now been more than four years since his trial, and for that entire time, apart from the occasional response, "Thank you for continuing to pray for our family," we didn't have a good answer to that question. Now, quite unexpectedly, there were tangible action steps people could put their energies into in order to provide much-needed help.

There are moments when you are living in your new kind of normal when you believe life can never be as good as it once was. But during the spring and summer of 2006, as family members and friends rallied around this gargantuan project, I could almost see the silver lining under the cloud of despair that always hovered in the background of our minds. We e-mailed our list of Stretcher Bearers and asked them to pray and write letters. The excitement was contagious, and our mailbox was full.

The first wave of mail came from people who collected signatures for the petitions asking the governor to fast-track Jason's case. A radio station in Fort Wayne, Indiana, put out an announcement regarding the need for signed petitions. We had lived in Fort Wayne when Jason was a preschooler, and old friends rallied around this project. The Advanced Writers and Speakers Association sent out an announcement that signatures were needed, and dozens of my colleagues gathered signatures at their speaking engagements. Individual conference and retreat groups where I had spoken contacted past participants and asked for help. Within less than three weeks, we had more than four thousand signed petitions in our hands!

Letters began arriving from people who were writing to the clemency board on behalf of Jason. We had hoped for three letters of recommendation from people who had served in elected positions, and that's exactly what we received—letters from two judges and a state representative. The letter from retired Circuit Court Judge Jerry Lockett was gripping. After reading about Jason's case in the newspaper, he visited Jason on several occasions. Judge Lockett was also a graduate of the U.S. Naval Academy and understood the kind of military training Jason had experienced just prior to the murder.

Dear Governor Bush,

. . . We all realize clemency is granted only under certain unique circumstances. In my opinion, this is one of the cases. The unfortunate homicide in this case was clearly in the heat of passion, and Mr. Kent should have been convicted of 2nd degree murder. Everyone understands what he did was wrong. From personal knowledge, I can assure the board that Mr. Kent is a man of high integrity and would not, in the future, harm anyone. He is extremely remorseful and could contribute a great deal to society. It would be appreciated if the board would grant him clemency or at least reduce his sentence to a fixed term of years. . . .

Respectfully yours,

Jerry T. Lockett

Additional letters came in as the word spread. Some of these were from professionals like Skip and Penni Tyler, chaplains in the police department:

Dear Members of the Executive Clemency Board,

As Chaplains within a paramilitary police organization, we deal with countless situations in which men behave in ways never thought possible. We are trained in dealing with Critical Incident Stress and Post Traumatic Stress, and we have an understanding of what happens within the mind at those critical points of trauma . . . It is always our desire to see justice served . . . However, in this case, we believe extenuating circumstances should be considered . . .

During the time before his crime, Jason Kent was under incredible stress due to his rigorous training at the Naval diving school. This stress was compounded by a very difficult situation in his personal life which pushed Jason's mental capacity to the limit. Jason clearly believed that his two stepdaughters were in grave danger from an allegedly abusive birth father. His concern for those children overshadowed all of his thoughts. With his stress level at maximum, coupled with his demanding military training, it is probable Jason's mind told him he must do whatever was necessary to protect those children, including employing his military training on some level.

Jason is most likely a victim of Critical Incident Stress. Unfortunately, no psychologist or psychiatrist specifically trained in the military mind-set was called to this situation at the crucial time when Jason's condition could have been deciphered. This diagnosis would have explained how a healthy, moral, law-abiding citizen could do something he would otherwise deem unthinkable . . .

> Respectfully Submitted,
> Skip & Penni Tyler
> Chaplains, Redding
> Police Department

The letter from my father was very personal.

My Dear Fellow Americans,
My name is Clyde Afman, age 83, World War II veteran,

European theater, 13th Armored Division, recipient of the bronze star. My wife Pauline and I have been married for sixty years, and we have raised six children . . . I have been a pastor for the past forty-six years . . .

Our first child, Carol Joy, has but one child, a son, Jason Paul Kent, . . . who has always been a high achiever and a compassionate man who loves God and his family. From early on he seemed destined for the military. He loved the navy and took pride in serving his country as a naval officer. Then tragedy struck.

You good and discerning people have a difficult responsibility to decipher truth from error . . . I plead for your mercy and compassion on behalf of a young man who has so much to give, who has an outstanding support base, and could make a tremendous contribution to his fellow man and to his country if given the opportunity. . . . My prayer for my grandson is that his life will not be wasted behind bars, but that one day (perhaps soon) he will be free to make a great investment in his family and in society . . . Thank you for considering this correspondence from an old man and a grandfather.

God Bless You,
Clyde Afman

It was still hard for us to wrap our minds around the dichotomy of our old normal, which included the pomp and pride of being the parents of a U.S. Naval Academy graduate, and our new normal, spending our free weekends inside a maximum-security prison. Uniforms were worn in both institutions—but that was the *only* similarity.

When the request for letters of support went out, we received two letters from men who were close friends of J.P. One was from his former USNA roommate, now Captain Chad Van Someren, U.S. Marines. The other was from Patrick McCrosky, a fellow inmate at Hardee Correctional Institution.

Chad's letter was on Marine Corps stationery:

Dear Governor Bush,

If ever there was a time for clemency, the time is now.

Jason Paul Kent has been justly sentenced for his crime. His sense of duty and obligation as a father to protect his family overwhelmed his normally good judgment. His crime was serious. His punishment is just.

Why clemency?

First, because Jason's guilt and remorse are real. He understands both the gravity of his crime and justice of his sentence.

Second, because Jason's conduct in prison has demonstrated a character of exemplary integrity. His positive outlook, his profitable use of time, his increased maturity (moral, intellectual, and emotional) reveal a man determined to make positive contributions to society.

Third, because Jason's positive contributions to society could be exponentially larger if he were free. This experience has been a defining experience for Jason. Far from being a threat to society, Jason's remorse is a springboard for a life dedicated to service; a rehabilitation of others—as he himself has been rehabilitated; a life dedicated to hope and second chances; a life characterized by both justice and mercy.

When used wisely, clemency is profoundly beautiful and

good. It takes into account character and compassion without minimizing the crime.

I shared a room with Jason for four years at the Naval Academy and respect him as a man of courage, character, and sincerity. I've visited him in prison and have kept in touch through letters. His remorse is real, his conduct is exemplary, and his future is bright.

Thank you for your consideration!

Semper Fidelis,
Chad Van Someren
Captain, U.S. Marines

Patrick's letter was handwritten on notebook paper from the prison commissary:

To Whom It May Concern:
I met Jason Kent while incarcerated with him at Hardee Correctional Institution. As a veteran of the U.S. military, having served six years in the navy, I was drawn to his natural leadership. Jason demonstrates daily the characteristics of an excellent leader and shows concern and compassion for other inmates.

Jason has been a strong Christian role model for me and for many others. When approached by other inmates who have personal, family, or court-related problems, Jason is quick to offer to pray with them. He rarely misses an opportunity to testify and evangelize. He selflessly offers his time to help other inmates with legal issues and with family-related struggles . . .

Jason has shared with me his desire to help inmates through opening a halfway house and a program designed to help convicted felons who are leaving prison to continue on the right path and to ensure they have the education, tools, and resources they need to remain out of prison . . . With the staggering number of inmates soon to be released from prisons . . . it is imperative that Jason Kent be granted clemency so he can begin to give back to society and help others in a way that few have the natural talent to do . . .

> Sincerely,
> Patrick McCrosky
> Inmate, Hardee Correctional
> Institution, Bowling Green, FL

HOPE RENEWED

After we began to gather petitions, letters, and documents for the potential of a clemency hearing, we were invited to the Florida Family Policy dinner in Orlando in May 2006. A new friend, founder and director of the International House of Hope, Sara Trollinger, invited Gene and me to be her special guests, and she made it possible for us to attend a predinner reception where we met Governor Jeb Bush, Attorney General Charlie Christ, and Tom Gallagher, the chief financial officer of the state of Florida. Admittedly, there were many hands for these politicians to shake that night, but we were infused with fresh hope knowing all three of those men were on the clemency board— and we had just met them in person!

It appeared God was opening every door and connecting us to people of influence who could help our son. I picked up my Bible and read: "Now may the God of hope fill you with all joy and peace in believing, so that you will abound in hope by the power of the Holy Spirit" (Rom. 15:13 NASB). I was beginning to believe we would have a chance at getting back some semblance of our old lives.

In all, we received close to one hundred letters of support from people who knew our family intimately or from professionals who understood Jason's case. As the mail continued to pour in, we photocopied the letters and sent them to Jason. Looking back, I know God used this time to give all three of us renewed hope.

One of Jason's phone calls during the weeks we worked on this project was particularly emotional. Overwhelmed with the time and care people took to write supportive letters on his behalf, J.P. said, "I feel like I'm reading my own obituary. Can you believe how gracious and kind people have been? I'm surprised they still remember me." He, too, was moved by the gigantic effort of so many people who wanted to help.

At that time, God reinforced some basic facts to Gene, Jason, and me:

- People still cared about encouraging us, even though it had now been almost seven years since the murder.

- Most people did not feel justice was served when J.P. received a sentence of life without the possibility of parole.

- God was still opening doors for all three of us to minister to others, and He had not forgotten us during our ongoing walk through a deep valley.

That week, I read these words from one of my favorite authors, J. I. Packer: "Hope generates energy, enthusiasm and excitement; lack of hope breeds only apathy and inertia . . . there needs to be hope in our hearts."[2] I could hear the voice of hope whispering in my ear, *Tomorrow will be better*. And I believed it!

THE PHONE CALL

It was July 13, 2006—more than four months since we started the process of seeking a place for Jason on the docket for the clemency hearing on December 6, 2006. Gene and I happened to be in Gene's office when the phone rang. Caller I.D. indicated the area code in which Tallahassee, the capital city of Florida, is located. My heart skipped a beat. I looked at my watch. It was 4:19 p.m.

"Oh, Gene," I sputtered as I ran to grab a second telephone so both of us could talk at the same time, "this could be the news we've been waiting for! This could be the answer to our prayers!"

After we picked up the receiver, the caller identified herself as legal counsel to Governor Jeb Bush. It felt like my heart was beating outside my chest. I couldn't believe we were getting a personal call from the office of the governor. This *had* to be good news.

She began, "The reason for this call is because our office received a personal request from the state representative in your district asking the governor to fast-track your son's case for a review by the clemency board." I could hardly breathe, I was so excited. "You are receiving this call as a courtesy to your representative. I have discussed your request with the governor, and Jason's case will not be fast-tracked because he is not desperately ill and he has not been incarcerated for a prolonged period of time. There are many cases ahead of your son's, and Jason's case does not merit fast-tracking."

My mind was blurring as Gene asked logical questions about the process and as he introduced mitigating circumstances we hoped would make a difference. I heard the woman say, "You need to understand what the clemency process *is* and what it *is not.* The clemency board has nothing to do with retrying a case. It has everything to do with mercy." Well, we certainly needed mercy!

As we neared the end of the call, I got up my courage to voice a question of my own. Calling her by name, I asked the governor's attorney, "What have we missed in this process that we should have done better? If Jason were your son, what steps would you take now?"

Her tone was professional and businesslike. "You've already done what you can. His case will be in the system, and it will eventually rise to the top, but of course that will be under another administration, because Governor Bush will be leaving office at the end of December." Then with a softened tone, she added, "Jason Kent has the best advocates any inmate could ever ask for. You have a wonderful family."

The call ended abruptly. Click. Over and out. The countless hours, multiple phone calls and e-mails, going to great lengths to get contact information for people we hadn't seen in several years, the gathering of petitions and letters—four months of nonstop work went out the window. Yes, his case would be "in the system," and it might rise to the top in twenty-four to thirty-six months, but the legal counsel had given us every indication Jason P. Kent hadn't begun to serve enough years to merit a clemency hearing yet.

Gene and I put both phones down. A terrible wailing sound was coming out of the depths of my being—a guttural groaning as I sobbed. I had not felt this depth of sadness since the day of Jason's conviction and sentencing. Gene was flushed, and I saw tears in his eyes too. We held each other for several minutes, unable to talk about the brief phone call that had shattered our hopes.

My intuition told me we shouldn't be alone the rest of that evening. But we didn't want to be with people we knew, because it was too hard to talk after such a major disappointment. I spoke up: "Let's go to Mimi's Café. We'll be around people we don't know, in a happy atmosphere, and maybe it will lighten our spirits."

The hostess at the café seated us in a booth. The young waiter took our orders. I was having trouble holding back tears. After our meal arrived, Gene took my hands in his, bowed his head, and began to pray, "God, we are so depressed! It seems nothing will work out to our son's benefit in this case. We're so discouraged. It appears that nothing 'good' ever happens no matter how hard we work and pray and wait. You seem to be at work in our situation, and then the door slams in our faces. Will our son ever see freedom again? Will he be in prison for the rest of his life? Please bring us some relief. We need hope. Jason needs hope. No one can go on living without hope. Oh, and please bless the food. Amen."

I could keep the floodgates closed no longer. The café provided cloth napkins, and I had no Kleenex in my purse. Gene immediately went to the men's room and confiscated toilet paper for his weeping wife. I was still holding the tissue in my hands when the waiter appeared once again to check on us. "Ma'am," he said, "if there's something wrong with the food, we won't charge you for this meal."

With puffy eyes and a red nose, I laughed aloud and said, "No, the food's fine. I'm just sad." It was good to laugh. It reminded me that I was still alive.

The teenager shrugged his shoulders and pivoted as he said, "Enjoy your meal."

RELINQUISHMENT IS HARD

In her book *As Silver Refined*, Kay Arthur says, "When we lose hope, in essence it's because we believe that God's lovingkindnesses have ceased—that there's nothing more we can expect from God, that He's reached His limit."[3] The night of the call from the governor's legal counsel I cried myself to sleep, still holding my wadded-up toilet paper from Mimi's Café. But morning came, and with it, fresh rays of sunshine streamed in my window and rippled over into my heart. I heard God whisper, *Carol, will you give this disappointment to Me? Will you lay it on the altar and trust Me with your son's future?*

I wish I could tell you that I immediately said, "Yes! And I am full of hope for my son's future, whether or not he ever walks in freedom again." After all, I wrote an entire book based on the story of Abraham and Isaac and reminded readers that Abraham had "history" with his God; he had so much faith and trust in God that he knew even if Isaac died on the altar, God would bring him back to life. I know the biblically correct responses. I'm a preacher's kid. I could probably quote all of the right chapters and verses to most questions about theological issues. I know them in my head. But believing them in my heart, seeing them shape my emotions—that's another matter.

That morning, I got on my knees and once again placed my will for my son on the altar. I felt as if it was sliding off the altar before I finished my prayer—but as honestly as I could, I said:

> *God, it seems terribly unfair that You allowed us to have so much hope for a clemency hearing for J.P., only to experience this crushing blow. I could handle it better if only Gene and I had to deal with the pain. But, Lord, Jason's hopes were so high that there might be the promise of a commutation of his sentence to a set number of years instead of a never-ending sentence. I can't bear to strip him of hope. And Lord, all of our Stretcher Bearers who have stood by us and prayed so long are expecting a miracle of mercy. God, I am disappointed in You. I'm hurting badly. But I still believe that nothing can touch us without Your permission, and so, today I'm laying my disappointment on the altar. I relinquish my expectations for a December clemency hearing for my son.*

I wish I could tell you I prayed that prayer of relinquishment and suddenly transformed into a woman with absolute trust in God for her son's future, but that wouldn't be true. I have to pray some form of that prayer every day, and sometimes multiple times a day. When you are living in a new kind of normal, relinquishment is an action step that often must be done daily as we get up, let go of our control over a person or a complicated situation, and move in a forward direction. It is never easy. It is never routine. It is hard work. But it is necessary.

MARY'S EXAMPLE

The mother of Jesus was the queen of relinquishment. When she and Joseph went to consecrate their son at the temple in Jerusalem, as Jewish law commanded, an aged saint who had been given prophetic insight entered with them and took Jesus in his arms. Simeon blessed the little family but also predicted that a sword would pierce Mary's soul because of her baby. "Simeon . . . said to Mary his mother, 'This child marks both the failure and the recovery of many in Israel, a figure misunderstood and contradicted—the pain of a sword-thrust through you'" (Luke 2:34–35 MSG).

God blessed me by not allowing me to know what the future held for our son. For the first twenty-five years of J.P.'s life, I did not have the kind of worries Mary faced from the very beginning of her pregnancy. To be told ahead of time that your son will be "misunderstood and contradicted" would have trapped many women in paralyzing fear. But not Mary. Her ongoing life of faith is evidence she relinquished that fear to the Lord.

A year or possibly two later, Joseph and Mary had to flee their homeland to keep their son alive:

After the scholars were gone, God's angel showed up again in Joseph's dream and commanded, "Get up. Take the child and his mother and flee to Egypt. Stay until further notice. Herod is on the hunt for this child, and wants to kill him." Joseph obeyed. He got up, took the child and his mother under cover of darkness. They were out of town and well on their way by daylight. They lived in Egypt until Herod's death. (Matt. 2:13–15 MSG)

This frightening story is well documented in Scripture. Herod was furious, and what he decreed is so disgusting it is hard to imagine the volume of the weeping of the mothers who lost their children at that time in history.

Herod, when he realized that the scholars had tricked him, flew into a rage. He commanded the murder of every little boy two years old and under who lived in Bethlehem and its surrounding hills. (He determined that age from information he'd gotten from the scholars.) . . . "
A sound was heard in Ramah,
> weeping and much lament.
Rachel weeping for her children,
> Rachel refusing all solace,
Her children gone,
> dead and buried.
(Matt. 2:16–18 MSG)

Mary, seemingly without complaint, relinquished her "right" to a normal life and fled her country to save the life of her child. But that was not her last move.

Later, when Herod died, God's angel appeared in a dream to Joseph in Egypt: "Up, take the child and his mother and return to Israel. All those out to murder the child are dead." Joseph obeyed. He got up, took the child and his mother, and reentered Israel. When he heard, though, that Archelaus had succeeded his father, Herod, as king in Judea, he was afraid to go there. But then Joseph was directed in a dream to go to the hills of Galilee. On arrival, he settled in the village of Nazareth. This move was a fulfillment of the prophetic words, "He shall be called a Nazarene." (Matt. 2:19–23 MSG)

Most mothers appreciate "roots"—that comforting feeling of being secure in your own home, knowing your family is safe and settled. Certainly during the early years of Jesus's life, Mary willingly released any claim to what many women today would call a "right."

By the time Jesus is twelve years old, Mary starts to experience what it will be like as her son begins to grow up and separate Himself from her in order to be who he was born to be. This is the beginning of another type of relinquishment for Mary. Their family makes their annual trip to Jerusalem for the Feast of Passover. When it was time to leave, Joseph and Mary assumed Jesus was with the group that accompanied them to the feast—but he was nowhere to be found, so they returned to Jerusalem.

The next day they found him in the Temple seated among the teachers, listening to them and asking questions. The teachers were all quite taken with him, impressed with the sharpness of his answers. But his parents were not impressed; they were upset and hurt. His mother said, "Young man, why have you done this to us? Your father and I have been half out of our minds looking for you."

He said, "Why were you looking for me? Didn't you know that I had to be here, dealing with the things of my Father?" But they had no idea what he was talking about. So he went back to Nazareth with them, and lived obediently with them. His mother held these things dearly, deep within herself. And Jesus matured, growing up in both body and spirit, blessed by both God and people. (Luke 2:46–52 MSG)

I believe this scene depicts Mary pondering about what the future will hold for her firstborn son. I wonder if she was beginning to realize there would come a time, perhaps sooner than expected, when she would need to relinquish Him once and for all, freeing Him to fulfill God's purpose for His life.

In Mark's Gospel, we're told that Jesus more or less rejects His skeptical mother and family and embraces His disciples as an alternate family (Mark 3:31–35). It had to be painful watching Him bring on Himself so much hostility from the religious establishment to the point where respected people accused Him of being possessed by the prince of demons (Mark 3:20–30). Mary lost her son yet again at the Crucifixion, got Him back from the grave for brief visits for a month, and then lost Him for the rest of her natural life at the Ascension.

Mary must have continually had to let go of that vision we discussed earlier in Luke 1:46–55 about what the Messiah would achieve, as the timetable kept getting pushed back. She died without seeing it completely fulfilled. She was a woman chosen by God for a job that could aptly be called "the mission of relinquishment." She had to practice a lifestyle of letting go— whether the issue was where she would live or protecting her son from His accusers. It had to be gut-wrenching.

My friend Lisa Ramsland also faced a complicated turning point early in her adult life.

LAYING A DREAM ON THE ALTAR

Growing up, I heard a Bible story out of Genesis 22 of a father named Abraham who was going to sacrifice his son Isaac because the Lord asked him to. I thought this was very scary, so I was relieved to hear that at the last minute, God provided a substitute for Isaac. Little did I know that in the future, God would be asking me to lay a dream on the altar. Similar to Abraham, I would have to choose if I would trust God.

By the age of four, I had accepted Jesus Christ as my personal Lord and Savior, and it wasn't long before I had committed to passionately pursue God's call on my life. At that age, I didn't care what it would cost. This commitment guided my thoughts and actions through my grade school and high school years.

As I stepped into a room to study for an exam my first year of college, I saw him. He was sitting at the head of the group, with the biggest blue eyes, an amazing smile, and a sense of peace and confidence that made me feel at home. I was awestruck. I had no clue that he could bring so many great memories and so much heartbreak.

The semester rolled on, and we ran into each other everywhere. We had the most delightful, deep conversations that I had ever had. In my daily quiet times, I questioned and pleaded with God for him to be the man I was to marry. Though my feelings grew as we developed a close friendship, he never asked me to be his girlfriend. Our relationship consisted of frequent phone conversations, e-mails, study times, and serving together at the same church. As I longed to have a future with him, I also knew in my heart that I had committed to put God first and sacrifice my own desires if they were not His plan for my life. When I transferred colleges, I laid the relationship on the altar and walked away crying.

At that same time, I sought God and His call on my life to serve in full-time ministry. I had the wonderful privilege of interning at a large church under the women's ministry director. At this point, I realized I was made to serve the Lord in a church and had a passion to help people grow deeper in their relationship with Jesus Christ. About a year later, I got a call from my college "friend" and recognized I still had feelings for him. He said he wanted to date me with the intention of marriage. He explained that during the last three years, he really did love and care for me but had not been ready for a relationship until now.

After an eight-month period of blissful courtship, we stood on a pier overlooking the ocean at sunset talking about the plans the Lord had put on our hearts. Before I could thank God for the conversation, he got down on one knee and asked if I would be his wife and serve God with him for the rest of our lives. I was so surprised that at first I did not answer, but a "yes" eventually came from my lips; then he kissed me for the first time. I had waited three years for that!

We planned to get married nine months later, after I graduated from college. As we made arrangements for the wedding and our life together, I was so happy. All the years of living for God felt worth it, and I had a great sense of peace. We entered premarital classes and counseling with confidence that our personalities, backgrounds, and values were in line and complementary with each other. Life was unfolding so nicely.

Four months into the engagement, however, I awoke one

morning with a feeling that something was wrong. I felt heaviness in my heart as a thick blackness seemed to invade my soul. Tears spilled from my eyes because the burden was so intense. I cried out to God to let it pass and asked that He would help me get out of bed, because this was the big day of wedding preparations with our families.

As my future in-laws along with my future brothers- and sisters-in-law rang the doorbell, I wished that my fiancé was there too, but he could not get the day off work. The plan was to try on bridesmaid dresses and tuxedos, meet with our wedding coordinator, and look at the church and reception hall. His dad was going to perform the ceremony, so we were going to go over the order of service. After months of hopeful planning, this particular day did not go well. Every discussion with my future family revealed a chasm in our convictions.

In the following months right up to sending out invitations, my fiancé and I had many conversations that revealed we disagreed on some of the most fundamental issues of family life. I was trying my best to stay afloat and convince myself that we would work things out. With each discussion, however, the waters became more impossible to navigate. Though my love for him was deep and my desire to walk in agreement was strong, I knew that I would have to give up God's call on my life to marry him. We both agreed that staying at home while rearing and educating children were high priorities. The difference was that I saw this as a season in a woman's life rather than a permanent job description. I was in love with this man, so my heart broke with the realization that I was not willing to pay the price it would take to spend my life with him.

In my heart, I knew that I had committed to passionately pursue God's call on my life, even if this meant sacrificing my own dreams. I wondered how Abraham could trust God that sacrificing his son was a part of the plan. That plan does not seem right! Where did he get his faith? But I knew the end of that story. How would my story end?

One of my last conversations with my fiancé took place in a parking lot and began with tears. He had no idea why I was crying, and I did not know the exact reason he was crying, but the sadness was there for both of us. In the midst of the agony, the Lord whispered to me, *Lisa, what are you going to do? Are you going to choose him or Me?* I could not believe it came down to this.

Driving home with tears streaming down my face, I pulled to the side of the road and told the Lord, "I choose You, even though it hurts deeply right now. I have no idea what plans You have for me, or if they will be better than being married, but I choose to trust You." A week later, I set both my fiancé and myself free from a life we both longed for but knew would never work.

It has been three years since that day, and the road has not been easy, but I am ministering full-time in a church, and God is blessing that. I cannot report that I have found another man to whom I am happily married. I do, however, know God in a new way, and my faith is stronger than it ever was before. Although I would love it if He happens to bring along another prince for me to marry, my faith and devotion to God do not depend on my circumstances.

As I continue to read the story about Abraham, I find his life was not blissful after he sacrificed Isaac either; he lost his wife. But the Lord blessed him. The Lord made his descendants as numerous as the stars in the sky. All of his offspring were blessed because He obeyed God. The Lord provides for what we need when we follow Him. I cannot wait to see what the Lord has in store for my life.[4]

THE HEART OF RELINQUISHMENT

Just like Lisa, I had to choose if I would display a heart of relinquishment. I like to plan an agenda, manage my schedule, and have a sense of direction that includes a reasonably predictable outcome. Most of us enjoy some spontaneity too—but nothing that makes us feel totally out of control. My life now is a strange dichotomy of predictability and uncertainty. Since Jason has a life sentence, one might think that our lives are easy to schedule. We know visitation days are on Saturdays and Sundays, and apart from a change in the prison rules, we'll be visiting our son in prison whenever we are free on weekends.

The uncertainty comes, however, because Gene and I will never stop being advocates for our son. We will never quit trying to find a way for our only child to one day walk in freedom. Trying to get Jason's case fast-tracked for a clemency hearing brought the exhilaration of having a goal that appeared to be achievable. Doing *something* feels so much better than doing *nothing* when a family member is in a difficult situation. Even if our efforts were no more productive than a gerbil's on a wheel, we felt as if we were at least trying to work out a plan that had the potential of success. However, when our plan fell into the realm of impossibility, the emotional pain was like a knife, cutting away at our hopes, punching holes in our dreams, and forcing us to crawl back on the altar called "relinquishment."

Recently, my husband's forty-seven-year-old brother was diagnosed with lung cancer. We haven't talked about what stage of cancer he is in; we just know it's serious and potentially life threatening. Monty and his wife, Sandi, not only care for their own children, but they are the legal guardians of Sandi's sister's five children (including triplet four-year-old boys) due to her sister's health challenges. As we watch them hold on to hope—while juggling chemotherapy, radiation, and a growing pile of expenses that are not covered by insurance—my heart cries, *Hello, God, are You there? Do You see how desperately this big family needs a father? We need a miracle!*

We don't know what the future holds for Monty or for our son, J.P. We want to control the outcomes of these stories, but they are not our stories to write. We are waiting "in the meantime" of life with no clear sense of direction and, at times, with dashed hopes.

This chapter began with wise words from Dr. Jack Hayford, and it seems fitting to quote them again: "Living with a miracle means far more than experiencing its conception. It means resting in God's promise and power even when it seems the miracle isn't going to be born."[5] That's where we are right now, in the "resting zone" of relinquishing our desires to the one who loves our family more than we do. For me, that means actively praying:

God, I release to You what I cannot control. I hold my son with open hands. The Bible says Your angels set up a circle of protection around us while we pray. I need that circle right now, not just for protection but for comfort. Lord, Mary didn't get to see the fulfillment of the vision You revealed to her. Will I be here long

*enough to see my son walk out of prison as a free man? Will
Monty live to see his children grow up? Or do You have a different
kind of miracle in mind for Jason, for Monty, and for us—not
the kind we're praying for but a miracle that's a better fit with
Your kingdom agenda? As I relinquish my control over my
dreams, I embrace Your new kind of normal for my life. Amen.*

GOD'S POWER IN YOUR
NEW KIND OF NORMAL

I have never met anyone who said, "Relinquishment is easy."
For most of us, making the choice to release our control over our
spouse, child, friend, job, or longed-for dream feels like someone
is prying our fingers open one by one and exposing our defense-
less hearts. Sometimes, when we have loss upon loss, we think
we *deserve* to be in control of certain outcomes, if only to protect
ourselves from additional hurt and pain. It seems the most irrational thing we can do is to let go one more time. We battle with
conflicting emotions and "duke it out with God," sometimes
through prayer, but occasionally by being obstinate. Our honest
thoughts reveal our deep fears: *So many bad things have happened to
me. How much more will God require? It seems irrational and unreasonable to
lay what is precious to me on the altar again.* Letting go of our grip on
predictable results and trusting God with our heart offering is
one of the most challenging choices we make.

1. When was the last time you had your heart set on a desired
   outcome (getting married, a confirmation of a pregnancy,
   being offered a dream job, receiving a good report on your

child's progress, a clean bill of health, etc.), but the situation did not turn out according to your plan? On a scale of 1 to 10, where were you emotionally? How does your emotional response impact your personal faith relationship with God?

2. The word *relinquish* has several synonyms. Decide which one you identify with the most:

- *Yield*—implies concession or compliance or submission

- *Resign*—emphasizes voluntary relinquishment or sacrifice without struggle

- *Surrender*—implies giving up after a struggle to retain or resist

- *Abandon*—stresses finality and completeness in giving up

- *Waive*—implies conceding or forgoing with little or no compulsion[6]

As you read through this list and considered which word best describes your current situation, did you believe one or more of these descriptions to be more "spiritual" or God-honoring than the others? Did that influence your decision, or did you feel comfortable selecting the one that fits where you truly are on your journey right now?

3. Reread Kay Arthur's startling observation: "When we lose hope, in essence it's because we believe that God's lovingkindnesses have ceased—that there's nothing more we can expect from God, that He's reached His limit."[7] Have you ever reached a discouraging point when you believed there was nothing more you could expect from God—that

your chance for His supernatural involvement in your place of uncertainty had run out? If so, what transpired to bring you to this place of hopelessness? Did this emotional state pass quickly, or are you still at a crossroads with your faith?

4. On page 149, I voiced an honest prayer of disappointment and relinquishment to God when I learned that my son would not get a clemency hearing. Following that prayer, I also reported that I have had to pray some form of that prayer every day since. Have you ever intentionally laid a person, situation, or hurt on the altar as you voiced relinquishment to God regarding your control of the person or state of affairs? Have you experienced permanent peace, or have you had to pray the prayer of relinquishment multiple times, much as I do?

5. Read again on pages 150-53 the story of Mary's multiple choices to practice relinquishment during different stages of Jesus' life. Do you think relinquishing Him at the cross was easier because she had already practiced relinquishment earlier in her life? How much of an eternal perspective do you think she had as she watched her son die on the cross? When she saw Him after the Resurrection?

6. Sometimes it's hard to combine relinquishment and hope in our personal circumstances—especially when nothing goes according to our plan. The Bible says, "Now may the God of hope fill you with all joy and peace in believing, so that you will abound in hope by the power of the Holy Spirit"

(Rom. 15:13 NASB). Think of a time when practicing relinquishment of your control over a person or a situation to God resulted in increased hope. That hope might have been for a brighter outcome in the not-too-distant future, or it might rest on an eternal hope that will not be fully realized until you leave this earth. If you feel comfortable doing so, call or write a close friend this week and share what you are learning about the combination of relinquishment and hope as you move forward.

seven

WHO'S TO BLAME?

When I Want to Point the Finger . . .
I CHOOSE FORGIVENESS

FORGIVENESS USUALLY ISN'T
A ONE-TIME EXPERIENCE.
IT'S AN ONGOING PROCESS.
YOU HAVE TO WORK AT IT.

—ELISA MORGAN

*E*ight years ago today, I was the mother of the groom. The weather was exquisite. The sun rose high in an azure blue sky, and billowing white clouds danced overhead in the late-summer breeze. It was as if heaven and earth celebrated this day with our family.

The ceremony was taking place in our hometown, so on the day before, our home became the central headquarters for out-of-town guests. It was also the place where meals were served (sometimes in rotating shifts) as relatives and friends came early to help with last-minute details and to arrive in time for the rehearsal. Our son and his fiancée were getting married. Their romance had blossomed in Florida, so most guests were meeting our soon-to-be daughter-in-law, along with our new grand-daughters, for the first time.

Excitement was flying high as my sisters, my mother, and other friends stuck their heads in my office (I was finishing last-minute work on the reception programs). The evening flew by. I looked at my watch. It was now approaching midnight, and most of the houseguests had gone to their rooms. But there was another task I had not yet done—and I dearly wanted to complete it before the next morning. My own mother had written a letter to me on the night before my wedding day, and I still treasure it to this day. I wanted to do the same for my son and his bride. Closing my office door, I wrote from my heart.

Dear Ones,

You will soon be united as one in marriage. I'm so happy for both of you, but my heart is filled with deep emotion. I'm saying good-bye to the little boy who filled our hearts with so much laughter, adventure, spontaneity, joy, and high energy. Son, I remember the day on Old Forge Drive when you were memorizing Romans 6:23 and you said, "Mom, what does that mean, that part about 'the wages of sin'?" That was the day you understood the gospel message and invited Jesus to be your Savior.

It was obvious from the start that you wanted a life filled with challenge, excitement, travel, and purpose. I watched God at work in your life when you attended Summit Ministries as a sixteen-year-old and gained a new perspective on what He might want to do with your leadership abilities. I wept when you came home and allowed me to read your journal. You were convinced that with God's help, one man could change the world, and you were willing to be that man.

Dad and I watched as you received an appointment to the U.S. Naval Academy. Your four years in Annapolis were filled with challenging physical and academic work, and I'm sure you know how proud your parents were—from Induction Day to Graduation Day! We know God is grooming you for a position of influence, and we are convinced you will reflect His glory in ever-increasing ways.

Now a beautiful woman has entered your life. She's the wife we prayed God would bring to you. During the past four years, in spite of the excitement of your academy experience and your last year in nuclear engineering school, I observed a deep lone-liness in you. I longed for you to find the wife of God's choos-ing who would bring joy, encouragement, tenderness, fun, and love into your life. It brings your dad and me great joy to see the two of you together—the laughter, excitement, affection, and companionship you share are obvious in one glance.

My precious daughter-in-law, I have prayed for you daily since Jason was in my womb. I didn't know your name, but God did. You are a gifted young woman, and it's a delight to observe your remarkable creativity and your artistic flair. I see a woman of personal integrity, love for God, and commitment to my son. I know my prayers have been answered. You are a fantastic mother, and God has blessed our lives with unexpected "grand-parenting joy."

There will be days when both of you are overwhelmed with pressure, and cross words may pass through your lips. Be quick to forgive each other and be aware that the enemy will always look for your most vulnerable weak point and zoom in for an attack. Dad and I were best friends long before we married. I'm glad your relationship started with friendship and a secure commitment to the Lord—complete in Him before you sought additional completion in each other.

You will be covered with prayer. Dad and I are here for encouragement, advice, love, and an occasional hearty laugh! We'll try not to interfere in your marriage, and we want you to know we look forward to many happy years with the four of you!

J.P., continue to treat your wife with gentleness, love, respect, and reverence. Put God first in your home and in your relationship, and you just have to be the happiest married couple this side of heaven.

Much love,
Mom

The next day I hand-delivered my letter, praying it would mean as much to its recipients as the letter from my mother had meant to me. That afternoon, as vows were exchanged and the ceremony took place, relatives and friends looked forward to seeing this young family thrive. This couple had everything going for them—a rich heritage of faith, the love and support of a large extended family, Jason's military career that would no doubt result in world travel, and two gorgeous little girls who filled every space they occupied with giggles and optimism.

WHAT WENT WRONG?

So how is it possible that I'm sitting here today with this same son sentenced to prison for the rest of his life? How could a story that began like a fairy tale have become such a nightmare? Some days are harder for me than others, and today questions storm through my mind.

God, we have tried to be faithful to You for our entire lives. We raised our son to love You and to respect others. How could You have let him murder another human being? He was covered with our prayers. Did You even hear our prayers? Does prayer make any difference at all? We tried to be good parents. We set boundaries and focused on character development. How could You allow this terrible thing to happen to our family? I feel angry with You for not stopping this crime before it happened. Our lives will never be the same. Our son has no hope of ever walking in freedom again. I know Jason has asked for Your forgiveness for his crime, this terrible sin that You hate, but it's hard for me to forgive You for not intervening in this situation before Douglas Miller Jr. died. I know you created man with a free will, but I also know You are sovereign. Right now I just can't put this theological mystery together in my head. I know You are omnipresent and omnipotent—
SO WHY DIDN'T YOU DO SOMETHING?

For a long time, I was too numb to recognize that I was pointing a finger at God for allowing this terrible thing to happen. Part of my mental and spiritual healing is taking place by admitting, first to myself and then to God, that I still struggle with forgiving Him. I think I forgive Him, but when nothing improves, I sometimes find myself blaming God for everything that's happened to turn my world upside down.

CHANGE UPON CHANGE

Following Jason's arrest, our relationship with his wife and stepdaughters became very close. All of us were functioning in a state of shock, and we desperately needed each other for comfort in the middle of such devastation. Even though we were in Michigan and Jason's family was in Florida, there were frequent phone calls as we began what eventually became a two-and-a half-year wait for a trial. In truth, we got to know the new loves in Jason's life much more personally *after* his arrest. Our depressing circumstances created a bond; shared pain drew us closer together.

Every Saturday night, our daughter-in-law faithfully took the girls to the Orange County Jail to visit J.P. Often the lines to get through security are long. The booths in the visitation area are filthy, and there is only one seat in front of each window. The Plexiglas between inmates and their visitors does not permit an embrace or any opportunity to hold hands. Our daughter-in-law was a trooper, trying to keep all of us encouraged. We always tried to call her after the visits, hoping to hear they had a meaningful time together and that J.P. was holding on to hope.

Following Jason's conviction, he spent six weeks at the Central Florida Reception Center going through testing to see where he would best fit within the prison system. Since half of all prison inmates are illiterate and less than 1 percent of inmates have a university education, they didn't have a great "placement program" for a U.S. Naval Academy graduate. We soon learned that Jason had been sent to Avon Park Correctional Institution in Avon Park, Florida. This prison had P.R.I.D.E programs on site. (P.R.I.D.E. is an acrostic for Prison Rehabilitative Industries and Diversified Enterprises.) At the Avon Park location, there is a tire recapping plant, a signs and graphics plant, and a cleaning supplies plant. Jason has outstanding computer skills, so he was placed in an office position, assisting the corrections officer who was in charge of the building where he worked.

In spite of an unending sentence, we anticipated a brand-new joy—being able to have one embrace when we arrived in the visitation area and one embrace when we said good-bye. After only one year of marriage and two and three-quarter years of separation due to incarceration, J.P. and his wife would finally be able to hold hands during their visits.

Jason's family had been living in a small rental north of Orlando that was an hour-and-a-half drive to the prison. Gene threw his energies into working with Jason's wife to find a home where the girls would be safe and where they would be closer to the prison so they could have regular visits with J.P. We finally decided it would be best if we copurchased a house to enable our little family to have enough space for the growing needs of the girls and to ensure they were able to live in a good neighborhood. It was only thirty-five miles to the prison.

After the exhaustion of moving, getting settled in a new home, and making sure the girls were on track with their homeschooling studies, Jason's family was now in a place where they had visits with J.P. in a much less restricted environment. The prison's visitation hours were on Saturday and Sunday, from 9:00 a.m. to

3:00 p.m., and Jason's wife faithfully made the trip to have these twice-weekly visits. This routine became their new normal. We knew there were some major challenges. Both our granddaughters wanted to play soccer, and the games were on Saturdays. They needed the exercise, and they needed interaction with other children. Most church services were on Sunday, but that was a visitation day with J.P.

Sometimes years tend to blur together as you live in a new normal. Jason's arrest was in October 1999. His trial was in April 2002. His placement in the Avon Park prison was in June of that year, and one year later the Department of Corrections mandated that inmates with a life sentence be placed in maximum-security prisons. Jason was moved to a facility in Bowling Green, Florida, a longer drive for his wife. Instead of being thirty-five miles away, she was now sixty miles from the prison where Jason was placed. At this facility there was no place for families to walk the perimeter of the visitation yard, and there were more guards watching every movement of the inmates and their guests.

Then came the summer of 2004, with all its hurricane-filled intensity. Three of four storms went through Hardee Correctional Institution (Jason's home) and right through the heart of the town where his family lived. Because the damage to the home was severe and there were not enough construction workers to cover the need during this intense time of multiple natural disasters, our daughter-in-law and granddaughters went back and forth between camping and insurance-supplied housing in area hotels. Now our son's wife faced the daunting task of homeschooling the girls out of a tent and/or a hotel, working with insurance adjusters, and conquering innumerable additional challenges that went along with the hurricanes that had wrecked havoc upon their lives.

Maximum-security prisoners were moved to other prisons so minimum security inmates could be moved into the Hardee prison in order to assist with hurricane cleanup. Jason was no longer living close to his family. That was a good reason for Jason not to get visits from his wife and stepdaughters during the six months' duration of his time at the Glades Correctional Institution near Miami, but eventually he was moved back to Hardee, which was a much shorter drive for his wife. I am not a psychologist, nor have I personally experienced the devastation of a woman who has gone through the kind of multiple knock-out punches Jason's wife received during a period of six and a half years—two miscarriages; a husband arrested, tried, and convicted for murder; multiple moves; three hurricanes; and the rigors of homeschooling. All I know is that stress has a high price tag, and visits to J.P. trailed off and eventually stopped in the spring of 2005.

At first we didn't know. Jason was very protective of his family and didn't mention for a long time that their visits had ceased. We had long before stopped calling on the evenings of visitation days, not wanting our daughter-in-law to feel we were checking to see if she was visiting her husband. It didn't feel right. Jason would occasionally mention that he received a letter from her or from one of the girls, which always pleased him greatly.

Suddenly, after two years on the market, our home in Michigan sold, and one month later, on July 1, 2005, we moved to Lakeland, Florida, about a thirty-minute drive from Jason's family. We immediately invited them over to see the new house and have dinner with us. Our daughter-in-law declined. Again and again she declined. We knew she was allergic to our cat, but we assured her we would keep him behind closed doors. She never came. We visited her and our granddaughters, but something was different.

Our daughter-in-law had decided to sell her house and move out of state, hoping for a chance to give her daughters a better, more normal life. In the brisk housing market in Florida during the summer of 2005, her home (which had now, a year later, been fully repaired) sold quickly. Gene and I told her we wanted her to have our half of the house, and we did not expect or want payment for our coinvestment in the home and for our half of the increased property value at the time of sale. We wanted her and the girls to be well cared for, and that was our gift to them. We told her that we understood the stress she was under and her desire for a different future for herself and for the girls, but we assured her we still wanted to be a part of her life, and we certainly wanted to continue being grandparents. Our daughter-in-law indicated it would be very hard to start over in a new place if we were involved in their lives.

We stopped by their house a few more times. Instead of having our beloved granddaughters run out the door and fly into our arms with glee, they ran to alert their mother that we were in the driveway. The discomfort was palpable, and the conversation was strained. Finally, the day arrived when the family was packed and ready to go. We asked if we could have their new address. Our daughter-in-law declined, saying mail we sent to them would be forwarded to her new address.

Our hearts were aching with the pain of saying good-bye to

our daughter-in-law and to our much-loved stepgrandchildren. The five of us awkwardly formed a circle, and we prayed for their safety as they moved to an out-of-state destination and a brand-new life. At this writing, it has been almost a year since we said good-bye, and we do not know where they live, nor have we heard from them. Christmas, birthday, and other holiday packages and cards have not been returned, so we pray the girls are aware of our continuing love and concern for them.

During the six years of close contact we had with the girls, we watched our six-year-old granddaughter go from a wide-eyed child of six to a budding teenager. Our cherubic-faced three-year-old who ran through our home chasing the cat has now turned eleven. I miss phone conversations with my daughter-in-law. Gene and I ache for contact with our grandchildren. We long for the privilege of giving them tangible encouragement and making sure that their needs are met. Jason is still married, so we are hoping for a miracle of restoration for this family we love so much. But right now we just wait and pray.

WHO'S TO BLAME?

It's easy to let seeds of resentment grow in our hearts and to cast blame. We've been hurt, and it feels as if we've been abandoned. But we realize that in our fervent desire to "help everything to be okay" for our son and his wife in the middle of a devastating ordeal, perhaps we were to blame by helping financially to buy them a home, inadvertently creating a sense of trying to manip-ulate a marriage into working. That wasn't our purpose, but that might have been the perception.

We were to blame for not talking about matters of the heart, when it was easier to pretend everything is eventually going to be fine. It wasn't, but we weren't ready to admit it to ourselves; much less did we feel ready to talk out loud about it to our daughter-in-law. Besides, deep down we were hoping one of the multiple appeals was going to produce good news—perhaps a new trial, or more recently, a chance at a commutation of Jason's sentence to a set number of years. We were wrong. We should have faced the hard issues of what our daughter-in-law was going through instead of trying to come in and sweep up the messy, complicated debris, perhaps behaving like white knights with occasional visits to break the monotony and never-changing nature of her life. We blew it. But we didn't mean to.

Part of me wanted to blame Jason's wife for not coming to us earlier with the news of how distraught her husband had become before the murder. We might have been able to do something then, but we were trying to follow biblical principles and let our son and his wife "leave and cleave." Perhaps we're the ones to blame for not being more involved in their lives during the first year of their marriage when the murder could still have been prevented. We just didn't know what was going on in Jason's mind.

We still don't understand why, after showering our daughter-in-law with love, tangible encouragement, and the amazing support of our Stretcher Bearers, she would turn her back, first on J.P. and then on us. But we were not walking in her shoes—watching her girls spend weekend after weekend in a prison visitation yard, with no hope of going to the beach as a family, going to the movies together, getting established in a local church, having a daddy at their soccer games—in other words, functioning as a "normal" family. We had pain, but we didn't have *her* pain. Our love could not take the place of a husband who was behind bars for a lifetime. It's hard, but we "get" that.

I thought of all of the ways we had at some point played the blame game.

- If J.P. hadn't pulled the trigger, our lives would not have been permanently altered in such a life-shattering way. How could he have done this horrible thing without thinking about what it would do to his wife and children, and to us? How could he have thrown his own life of freedom away and destroyed life as we knew it in an irreconcilable way?

- How could our daughter-in-law have taken the girls, left Florida, and not given us a forwarding address? To lose Jason to prison has been unthinkable, but to lose our daughter-in-law and simultaneously, our only grandchildren, has been another devastating blow.

- How could the prosecutor close her eyes to Jason's true heart and not offer a reasonable plea bargain to a man who believed he was protecting innocent children? She knew it was his first and only offense, and she often offered plea bargains to hardened criminals. Why not in this case?

- How could the State of Florida rubber-stamp every appeal at every turn with a rejection? Are they so used to saying no that they don't even read the paperwork? This case *is* different from a typical murder case, but Jason has the same sentence as Charles Manson and the terrorist Moussaoui. Where is the fairness in *that?*

- How could God allow us to put four months of nonstop effort into fast-tracking Jason's case for a clemency hearing—only to allow our hopes to be decimated *again*?

Archibald Hart wrote, "Forgiveness is surrendering my right to hurt you for hurting me."[1] Forgiveness means to give up our resentment for the omission or commission of something that hurts us. Forgiveness grants relief to the person who "owes" us for what they have done to us or allowed to happen to us. In its most complete form, true forgiveness means we cease to feel resentment against the person who inflicted the pain.

The easiest person for me to forgive is my son, because every time I visit him I can see the permanent bondage he faces. He understands what he has done to himself, his family, the family of the deceased, and to us. I believe that when he committed the act of murder, he had the mind of a military warrior who believed he was saving his stepdaughters from potential harm. That didn't make his actions right, but it made me want to investigate how we train our military men and women to do the unthinkable for the cause of freedom while not understanding how that training might trickle down to a family situation that a young, inexperienced officer perceives as "imminent danger." In fairness to the military community that I respect and appreciate greatly, it's important to point out that the military *does* provide specific training designed to prevent the armed forces from blurring their roles in the military with their roles as private citizens. All of this is complicated to me even today, but it makes it easier to forgive J.P.

I think I have forgiven everyone else on that list—at least I have verbalized that to God—but there are days when an incident triggers my desire to blame someone else, and I have to ask God for forgiveness again. As we were driving through Orlando on I-4 recently, I saw the tall building that is easily recognizable as the courthouse. Waves of painful memories swept over me as I thought back to the most difficult week of my life. I could feel my resentment toward the prosecutor rearing its ugly head. That thought was followed by fresh anger at the media for wanting to sensationalize our family's pain during our most vulnerable hour. After assuming those thoughts were behind me because I had already voiced my forgiveness of those people in a prayer, I was surprised with their intensity. I had to pray that prayer again—and several times since. I'm learning that forgiveness is a lifetime process, not a one-shot cure-all.

There is probably no one I know who is more honest and straightforward than my husband. He writes his feelings down more often than I do. I think it's his way of continuing to cope with the sadness of Jason's incarceration. He wrote the following about forgiveness:

I have not felt the need to forgive anyone in all of this. Maybe I'm still processing and will suddenly, one day, be struck with the need to forgive someone, but not yet. Where would I even begin? Do I need to forgive society for allowing bad things to happen without stopping them? Do I need to forgive my daughter-in-law for telling J.P. about the abuse and hurts of her past? But that's what married couples do—they share their pain. Do I need to forgive the church for not helping young couples cope with marriage more wisely? Do I need to forgive Jason, my son, for being such an idiot in handling this difficult situation? Perhaps I need to forgive the military for putting so much stress and pressure on their soldiers. I may need to forgive myself for not teaching my son better coping skills. Or forgive myself for not communicating more with my son after marriage and for not asking more hard questions. Or forgive myself for not intervening more. I don't know where forgiveness begins or ends.

Perhaps I need to ask for forgiveness—from my son, my wife, my daughter-in-law, my granddaughters, and everyone for not seeing what was going on.

In certain ways, and at sporadic times, I've done all of the above, but it doesn't really help. Almost nothing helps with the pain of seeing my son in a prison uniform instead of his naval uniform. Nothing helps with the lost hope for his future and his lost dreams. Every time I visit the prison, I wonder how this could have happened—and it's been almost seven years! Won't there be an end to it? I know there is no good answer, so I just throw all of it in some dark corner of my mind and try not to think about it. I immerse myself in reading, in exercising, in working, in helping other people out, in encouraging my wife—and I try to forget the pain.

I realize that every psychologist who reads this book may want to put Gene and me in therapy immediately—but in some miraculous way, we're doing okay. We're not *fine*. We're not *happy* with our circumstances. But we're not living in denial or bitterness either. We're just trying to be honest about how hard forgiveness is. It's difficult to understand and it's difficult to practice. We can set an intention to forgive, but it is a sticky process with many twists and turns, especially when we are still being hurt.

THE ULTIMATE FORGIVENESS

On the cross, Jesus said, "'Father, forgive them, for they don't know what they are doing.' And the soldiers gambled for his clothes by throwing dice" (Luke 23:34 NLT).

After what He had just been through, a statement like that seems unthinkable. Men that His Father had created were mocking Him. How could He push up on the nails in His feet, sending excruciating pain throughout His body, and get the breath to audibly forgive these people for such atrocities? His situation was not only unfair; it was humiliating, despicable, and sickening. But He forgave them.

What must have gone through Mary's mind when she heard that her son had made this plea on behalf of the men who tortured Him? It's hard to imagine a mother not wanting revenge, especially a mother who was attuned to the injustices her people had been suffering for so long. The temptation to hate the Romans or the high priests would have been overwhelming.

Or perhaps Mary's mind went back to the scene when her son was twelve years old as He responded to hard questions in the temple, and she pondered in her heart what had transpired. Surely she understood that He was born for a mission that would produce forgiveness and salvation for all who would call on His name. But could she comprehend the heinous process He would have to endure? How much did Mary know about what would be required of her son, the Messiah, during her lifetime?

We don't have those answers in the Bible, but Scripture is full of reminders of the importance of true forgiveness:

- "But if we confess our sins to him, he is faithful and just to forgive us our sins and to cleanse us from all wickedness" (1 John 1:9 NLT).

- "Be gentle with one another, sensitive. Forgive one another as quickly and thoroughly as God in Christ forgave you" (Eph. 4:32 MSG).

- "'Master, how many times do I forgive a brother or sister who hurts me? Seven?' Jesus replied, 'Seven! Hardly. Try seventy times seven'" (Matt. 18:21–22 MSG).

I love that last verse because it reminds me Jesus knew that forgiveness, for most of us, is a process that often has to be repeated, not a one-time decision that lasts a lifetime.

Sandra Troutman knows what I'm talking about. I first met her in Seoul, South Korea, where I was speaking for Faithlift, a women's conference for military wives and active duty women in the military. Four hundred women gathered in the chapel at Yongsan Military Base for spiritual encouragement and mutual strength. Sandra's husband was deployed a couple of years later, and during that time she came face-to-face with the challenge of forgiveness.

A DIFFICULT SUNDAY

It was Father's Day. Mark was in Iraq, and we had grown to dread the holidays alone without him. Still, my young son and I determined to go to church. When it was time for Nathan to go forward for the children's message and then on to children's church, he did not want to go. This was unusual for him, because he loved going to children's church, but he is also tender and good. I knew that he was staying in the pew with me so that I would not have to be alone.

During the children's message, the kids were given baskets of gifts and asked to go out into the congregation and give one to each dad sitting there. When the little girl came to our pew, Nathan leaned across to be handed a gift for his dad. The little girl's eyes opened wide and she silently shook her head no. When he persisted, she whispered, "You can't have a gift because you don't have a daddy with you." I winced at her words as I gently leaned out and explained to her that Nathan's daddy was in Iraq and that he would like to send him the gift.

Reluctantly she loosed her grip on the clear-wrapped pen and let me take it. Nathan clung to that pen during the entire service. After the congregation was dismissed, we followed our usual procedure of walking to the fellowship hall for coffee and doughnuts and to visit with friends. We stood against the wall, and to my stunning amazement, no one spoke to us—*no one in the entire room even greeted us.*

I knew these people well, and they knew me. I had been actively involved in this church since we moved to the area. I counted some of the people in that room among my dearest friends. But this was Father's Day, and I had become a single woman standing alone with a child. And no one knew what to do with us. We had become invisible. Nathan and I left the church that day in silence, his hand tightly slipped into mine.

Father, I silently cried out through my tears, *how do I explain this to Nathan? Father, we came to Your house today needing to find hope and comfort. We miss Mark so much, and being without him has been harder than we ever dreamed. I cannot believe we stood there and were invisible to an entire church.*

We got into the car, with my soul continuing to rage in stunned disbelief, and drove home silently. Quietly from the back-seat, my precious seven-year-old spoke. "Mom, are you okay?"

It took me weeks to go back to church. But God opened my eyes to something that day. I kept thinking about James 1:27, which says, "Pure and undefiled religion, in the sight of our God and Father, is this: to visit orphans and widows in their distress . . ." (NASB). I wondered how many "orphans and widows" stood among us, invisible. As a church, have we turned a blind eye to the hurting or different? Do we not really *want* to know or see anyone or anything that might shake us from our comfortable position? Has church become a place where, for a brief moment in time, we can feel good and lovely and perfect and we do not have to be reminded that our world is a broken world and that people around us might be wounded and in need?

I have grown to believe that real love is love that sees and loves still. How many invisible people are standing right there beside us with their excruciating pain and sorrow and loneliness and are wholly ignored because they threaten our own comfort and reality?

I grew to understand that the people who did not see Nathan and me that day are broken and frail too. Scripture is clear that we all "fall short of the glory of God" (Rom. 3:23). And I determined to see their brokenness and to try and love them, as I want to be seen and loved in my own brokenness. I needed to forgive them in my heart for making us invisible on a day when we most needed their support.[2]

PRACTICING FORGIVENESS

Forgiveness is not forgetting the pain, nor is it approving of the wrong actions of others. Forgiveness does not erase the memory of what has happened, nor does forgiveness mean everything will turn out okay. There are still many times when I identify with the psalmist: "I've cried my eyes out; I feel hollow inside. My life leaks away, groan by groan; my years fade out in sighs. My troubles have worn me out, turned my bones to powder" (Psalm 31:10 MSG). But I continue to learn that forgiving is a choice that brings healing—probably more to the giver than to the recipient. When we forgive, we do not change the circumstances or injustices of the past. What we change is the future—for ourselves and for the ones we have forgiven. It is the most freeing choice we can make.

Some days, Gene and I blame ourselves for not being better parents. On other days, we seek forgiveness for all of our self-condemnation. On some days we blame God, and on other days we thank Him for His mercies, which are new every day we continue to walk this bumpy road (Lam. 3:22–23). We're simply trying to be real about blame and forgiveness. And it's very complicated. We have each other, and that's good.

GOD'S POWER IN YOUR
NEW KIND OF NORMAL

When we are not as happy as we'd like to be, it's easy to play the blame game. We look around and try to find someone or something we can hold responsible for causing our problem. Once we identify a potential cause—especially an individual who "should have known better," we begin mentally listing our "justifiable" reasons for pointing a finger at the cause of our pain.

God must have known it would be hard for us to forgive, because that topic is mentioned throughout the Bible and it's even included in the Lord's Prayer: "And forgive us our sins, just as we forgive those who sin against us" (Luke 11:4 NLT).

As Gene and I continue to live in a very unlikely place, we find that we hadn't realized how many people we would need to forgive in the process. The most subtle forgiveness challenge we faced was forgiving God for allowing such a horrible thing to happen. No doubt you, too, have encountered forgiveness issues that are intricately woven into your own realigned version of "normal."

1. Read through this list of ways people respond when they have been wronged. Which one best describes your reaction when someone needs your forgiveness?

- I tend to hold grudges a long time.

- I usually quit "finger pointing" after a period of time, but I like the offender to know that he or she has wronged me and I'm not happy about it.

- I relive the grievance repeatedly and allow bitterness and resentment to develop—especially if the offender has been a real jerk and isn't repentant at all.

- My response depends upon how bad the action of the other person was. I believe certain actions shouldn't be easily forgiven.

- I let go of my hard-heartedness toward a person or a situation fairly soon but not immediately.

- I instantly forgive others because I have been forgiven.

2. Have you been in a situation where you verbally forgave someone who asked for your forgiveness, but you discovered there was still resentment in your heart? Did you go back and discuss your unforgiveness with that individual, or did you just talk to God about it? Have you ever been the one who needed to request forgiveness for a wrong action or attitude? If yes, what was the result?

3. Read through the following Scriptures. Write down one thing each verse teaches about forgiving someone who has wronged us.

- "Don't repay evil for evil. Don't retaliate with insults when people insult you. Instead, pay them back with a blessing. That is what God has called you to do, and he will bless you for it" (1 Peter 3:9 NLT).

- "Forgive as quickly and completely as the Master forgave you. And regardless of what else you put on, wear love. It's your basic, all-purpose garment. Never be without it" (Col. 3:13–14 MSG).

- "Do not repay anyone evil for evil. Be careful to do what is right in the eyes of everybody. If it is possible, as far as it depends on you, live at peace with everyone. Do not take revenge, my friends, but leave room for God's wrath, for it is written: 'It is mine to avenge; I will repay,' says the Lord" (Rom. 12:17–19).

4. Have you ever had an experience when it appeared that in spite of trying to do all the right things, and even though you prayed for a person or a situation for a long time, you saw no evidence of God's help or intervention? Did you ever struggle with overt or even subtle anger toward God? If so, read through the responses below and identify where are you right now in your relationship with God:

- I'm angry with Him for not intervening in my situation.

- I'm baffled at what seems like silence from God when I have sought answers through His Word and through prayer.

- I think He's busy elsewhere with global concerns and He doesn't involve Himself in "the small stuff" connected to my personal life.

- I believe God's timing is always perfect, and even though I may not understand why my prayers have not been answered the way I wanted, He has a better plan, and I'm trusting Him.

- Even when I'm tempted to question God for what He has allowed to happen in my life, I know He loves me and I do not hold unforgiveness in my heart toward Him. (If you selected this response, how long does it take you to get to this level of trust?)

5. Mark Twain once said, "Forgiveness is the fragrance the violet sheds on the heel that has crushed it."[3] He indicates there is a powerful and positive side to forgiveness that benefits the one who offers genuine forgiveness. What do

you think the benefits are to the person who extends complete forgiveness? Do you think the rewards are only spiritual, or are they physical too? Have you experienced any of these benefits? If so, explain.

6. Think of a time when it was hard for you to forgive another person for what he or she did to you or allowed to happen. Did you surrender your right to hurt someone else for hurting you? Did you hold resentment toward that individual for a long time? If you have come to a place of forgiving that person, write him or her a letter expressing your current response in light of what God is teaching you. If your resentment is toward God, write Him a letter in the form of a prayer. Even if you are not at a place of being able to forgive Him right now, you can express your honest questions and you can communicate your frustrations. You can tell Him anything, and He will not be angry with you!

eight
PITY PARTIES, DREAMS GONE AMUCK, AND NEW BEGINNINGS

When I Want to Give Up . . .
I CHOOSE PURPOSEFUL ACTION

PURPOSE IN LIFE IS NOT JUST SOMETHING WE DO.
IT INVOLVES WHO WE ARE
AND OUR WAY OF BEING IN THIS WORLD . . .
OUR HEART IS BROKEN BY WHAT BREAKS GOD'S HEART,
AND WE DEVOTE OUR ENERGIES TO THOSE PURPOSES.

—JAN JOHNSON

The phone rang. Gene answered and then called, "Carol, hurry, get on the line! It's Ginger and Anne—they just left the hospital!" I had known these friends for twenty years, and they were calling with celebratory news.

"The baby is here! Little Liam was born yesterday. He's so adorable, and he has lots of dark brown hair! Michael and Allison are exhausted but ecstatic. We both just became grandparents—

on the same day!" The excitement in their voices was euphoric as they passed the cell phone back and forth in the car.

I had met Ginger and Anne years earlier when Ginger lived in California and Anne lived in Canada. Both of these gifted women had eventually become a valued part of the teaching team for the communications training seminars I present in many cities each year. My mind flashed back to the year Ginger and Anne brought their sixteen-year-old children to a Speak Up with Confidence Seminar we were presenting at a charming conference center near Hillsdale, Michigan.[1] The setting was pastoral as 250 forested acres merged into the spring-fed waters of Weatherwood Lake. After three days of intense work with seminar participants, it was time to pack up and head for home—but no one could find Anne's daughter, Allison, or Ginger's son, Michael.

We already knew Michindoh Ministries Conference Center was the perfect place to explore nature and experience the out-doors, but as it turned out, it was also the ideal location to fall in love. Michael and Allison were eventually discovered on the dock overlooking the lake, holding hands and saying tearful good-byes. Eventually, these two dynamic, academic-minded Christian teenagers went to separate universities, and six years later, the love that was sparked at a conference center in the woods led to a chapel where they promised to love each other for the rest of their lives. It was a fairy-tale love story.

My friendship with Ginger and Anne was deep, and it had been forged during our good times and our bad times. They were there for me during the start of our emotional journey when Jason was arrested and eventually tried and convicted. After their children married, I had witnessed their heartbreaking journey through

Allison's multiple miscarriages. Michael and Allison had longed for a baby—and now, on this glorious spring day, they had witnessed the birth of their first child, born to a woman who loved her baby enough to release him for adoption. Their joy was tangible for the new parents and for the grandparents.

As I listened to the voices of much-loved friends describe the details of the birth, the activities at the hospital as the families gathered, and the exhilaration of Michael and Allison, I wept. The call ended on a high note. I was thrilled for my friends and for their children!

But the tears wouldn't stop. I started sobbing.

"What's wrong with you?" Gene asked.

I blubbered, "I'm so happy for them!"

"So why are you crying?" my mystified husband questioned.

My sobs got more intense and intentionally dramatic now that I had a one-man audience. "Because I'm so sad for myself! They have what I want—a happy family celebrating normal things, like childbirth and big dreams for the future. They'll be going on trips with their kids and celebrating holidays around a barbecue pit or a Christmas tree—and we're never going to have that. I'm so jealous! I wouldn't take it away from them for a minute, but I want it too. We've been through so much grief. Didn't we raise our son as well as they raised their children? I *deserve* to have a pity party—so just leave me alone and let me be miserable!"

Gene left the room, knowing by now how important it was for me to be alone sometimes so I could have a good cry. In some mixed-up way, I knew he understood how genuinely happy I was for Ginger and Anne—but that I just needed a little personal grieving time.

LOST DREAMS

Dreams are made of strongly desired goals for the future or the fulfillment of an intensely desired purpose. Dreams have to do with satisfying our wishes for something good. Without dreams, we begin to wither up and die emotionally.

In the beginning of our journey with Jason, even though the circumstances were devastating, for two and a half years prior to his trial, we had the hope of a plea bargain and the dream of a future for our son outside of prison. After his conviction, we kept our dream alive by going through the multiple-step appeal process. When we ran out of options for appealing at the state level, along came the dream of the possibility of obtaining a clemency hearing while Governor Bush was still in office. When the possibility of that dream vanished, Gene and I had to acknowledge our lost dreams of ever having a normal future for our family and talk to each other about them.

We listed some of the significant events and changes in our lives since Jason's incarceration:

- Our nephew, K.C., got married and was sent to Iraq with the marines. Jason loved the military, and now one of his cousins was deployed. We knew, in spite of the danger, that this assignment was exactly what J.P. would have loved doing for his country.

- Eight of J.P.'s other teenage cousins graduated from high school and began their university studies. Four of them have already graduated, and two are currently in law school. All of them are following their dreams of using their education in productive ways. In some ways, we live vicariously by watching them flourish.

- Gene and I transitioned from being highly involved grandparents to uninvolved grandparents. There is no more playing dress-up with Grammy's nightgowns, silk scarves, jewelry, and high heels. Our exuberant dancing girls are gone, and our sorrow is great.

- We spend almost every holiday inside a maximum-security prison with our son.

In other words, life is going on all around us, and family members and friends are living out their normal lives—while we are still adjusting.

Recently Gene shared with me some of his written reflections on what his new normal is like.

My most difficult time with my son in prison is right after I say good-bye to him. Upon leaving the visitation area, reentering my I.D. number on the keypad, having my hand imprint recorded, going back through the loud, staggered lockout doors, passing through the metal detectors, and walking beneath the razor wire, the devastation of this situation hits me anew. What must it do to J.P. as he goes back to his cell?

I unlock my car, open all the windows, and let the hot Florida air blow through the vehicle. And then the thought hits me like a fist: What does it all mean? My son has been sentenced to life in prison, and this is all we will have to look forward to for the rest of our lives: visitation with him at the prison.

My mind spins. Who will care for Jason's needs if his wife leaves him and we are no longer alive? Who will take care of our son's needs then? Who will work on any possibility of a commutation of his sentence to a set number of years instead of a "forever" sentence? Who will put money in his account so he can buy toothpaste, shaving cream, and shampoo? Who will arrange for people to visit him? Will there still be people who care about him ten years from now? Twenty years from now? Thirty years from now?

All of these thoughts don't weigh down my every waking moment, but they are always in the recesses of my mind. It is as if the "incident" that turned our lives upside down is a silent mistress that requires all my energy and concentration without giving anything back in return.

One day after visiting J.P., I found myself stopping at the corner grocery store on the way home. I parked and roamed the aisles for junk food. It's like I subliminally thought I deserved a reward for enduring this never-ending situation. I looked for cookies—not just any kind, but crunchy cookies. During my hunt, I discovered a special on Famous Amos Chocolate Chip Cookies—buy one package and get a second package free. What a deal! I immediately went to the checkout and took my contraband home.

I walked in the back door and poured cold milk in a large coffee mug and placed fifteen cookies on a plate. One by one I dunked the cookies and ate them all, ruminating over my sorrows. I went back for more and polished off an entire package of those cookies in one sitting.

I'm sure drowning my sorrow in cookies and milk is not any different than the pleasure of a drink of alcohol, or drugs, or whatever addictive behavior numbs pain for other people. I should have come home and worked out hard or cleaned the yard, or tried jogging, or read my Bible—but sometimes I have no desire. I know intellectually and spiritually that God still loves me and He loves my son and that He can use all this for good. But for a few moments I don't care.

I must admit I don't throw a pity party and binge on cookies after every visit. On most days, I have perspective. I'm discovering the best way for me to deal with my depression is to be involved with helping someone else. Whenever I can take my eyes off myself and off my problem, I find purpose again—and in that process I find unexpected joy.

As I read Gene's straightforward thoughts, it is a reminder that, humanly speaking, there are many days when it appears our lives are in the dumpster—but God! His name stands for redemption, salvation, hope, faith, strength, and courage. He is a God of new beginnings—and that's exactly what He has offered to us.

OUR NEW NORMAL

Author and speaker Jan Johnson says, "If we value our suffering and let it reshape us, our purpose can be forged ever stronger as we choose peacefulness and hope over bitterness and despair . . . (God) asks that each of us cooperate with the force of His fingers and the nudges of His voice to become vessels He can use."[2]

Gene and I have not yet figured out the mysteries of the sovereignty of God—in the universe or in our lives. However, we are trying to cooperate with the nudge of His voice as we choose purposeful action in our new set of circumstances.

One day, I started to itemize some of the positive choices we've made since Jason's conviction.

We made friends with others who are on a similar journey. After prison visitation one Sunday afternoon, we invited Candi, her five-year-old twin boys, and her mom over for dinner. Their daddy is incarcerated in the same prison where J.P. is located, and he has another seventeen months to go before he is released. Our shared pain creates a bond, and the friendship developed quickly. In the past, we didn't know any families of inmates; now we know several. Our lives have been enriched by sharing in the anguish of Candi and her boys, along with many others.

We joined a new church. We have lived in Lakeland, Florida, for more than a year, and a common question we are asked in our travels is, "Have you found a new church yet?" The truth is, on weekends when I'm not speaking on a Sunday, we often get home from weekend ministry trips between midnight and 2:00 a.m. on a Sunday morning, and Sundays are visitation days at the prison. There's one church in town that has an 8:00 a.m. service, but if we attend, we don't arrive at the prison until midmorning—and visits are the greatest encouragement we can give to our son.

One day I looked at Gene and said, "We *do* have a new church! It's The Church of the Razor Wire." We aren't allowed to talk to other inmates, but our parishioners are their moms and dads and wives—the ones we stand in interminable lines with as we prepare to go through security—and many of these folks are dynamic Christians. One of our congregants is Cliff, the inmate who works at the food window. Then there's another Jason who takes Polaroid snapshots of inmates with their families during visits. And let's not forget the corrections officers we interact with regularly, especially those who have forgotten how to smile, show respect, and voice a kind word. (I've recently discovered two guards who are Christians.) So, this *is* our church. For this season of our lives, this is a significant place of ministry. We are intentionally choosing to reach out to our new "church family." They enrich our lives, and we are able to pour kindness and hope into theirs.

We launched Speak Up for Hope. This nonprofit organization assists churches and individuals in working with prisons to provide hands-on encouragement to inmates and their families. Last spring the women's ministries director at Johnson Ferry Baptist Church in Marietta, Georgia, organized a large group of women to fill fifty "Boxes of Hope" that were sent with handwritten notes of encouragement to mothers and wives of inmates all over the country. These gifts were delivered just before Mother's Day, and the joy-filled responses from the recipients were heartwarming. Penny Williams, a psychologist from Michigan, volunteered to write Speak Up for Hope workbooks for support groups for families and friends of inmates. Church groups have sent coloring books, crayons, games, and educational flash cards that we have shipped to multiple prisons for their visitation areas.[3] We are realizing Speak Up for Hope gives back to us as we give to others, adding life-giving encouragement and surprising purpose to our lives.

We chose not to waste our lives because life didn't turn out the way we wanted. Our greatest temptation has been to quit ministry, give up our dreams, start a franchise called Pity Party Supplies, and withdraw into self-absorbed misery. The spiritual empowerment we receive by choosing to move in a forward direction is much like Joseph must have felt when he said to his brothers: "You intended to harm me, but God intended it for good to accomplish what is now being done, the saving of many lives" (Gen. 50:20). Only we're not saying those words to family members; we're yelling them in a megaphone in the face of the enemy. He is a loser—he just doesn't "get it" yet. We are *not* giving up on God!

We refused to hide in fear of being "found out." Every week we meet people who whisper their deep, heart-wrenching "secret" to us— their father is in prison, or they were abused as a child, or they have been divorced multiple times, or they have been diagnosed with bipolar disorder, or their brother is a convicted sex offender, or they are struggling with an addiction, or they have lost their faith in God. Gene and I have become convinced that when people refuse to be authentic enough to speak about their personal challenges, even to one other person, it will be impossible for them to fully embrace their new kind of normal and move in the direction of a purpose-filled life. When we began to honestly share our own journey with others, we discovered the whole world is desperate for somebody to say, "My life is a mess, and I'm trying to survive too! I'm struggling, I'm hurting, and I have questions about my faith. May I talk to you?" Being authentic has been our most important step in choosing purposeful action and in finding meaningful ministry.

JASON'S REFLECTIONS

Our son is living in a place where many of the inmates around him have innumerable tomorrows—because many of them have been sentenced to life without the possibility of parole. He recently said, "Mom and Dad, the lengths of their sentences allow them to put off good reading, exercise, personal goal setting, and any urgency connected to doing a job (which they don't get paid for) well. They always have 'another day,' so procrastination becomes the mantra of their existence."

I asked J.P. to write about how he chooses purposeful action in the midst of an endless sentence.

When I was at the U.S. Naval Academy, running started out as a duty, a responsibility to the men I would be leading, a mandatory period of painful preparation for a tough future job. But as I became stronger, I focused less on overcoming the pain and fatigue of my legs and summoned my will to make it another mile and more because of the opportunity it provided to get me away from the major distractions and agenda items I faced every day. I was able to focus, instead, on where I stood with God, what He wanted to do with my life, and whether or not I would trust Him with my future.

As the years went by, I would hit the beach and run for miles, or I'd choose the rough terrain of the woods or the mountains. Initially, I was driven to temper my body and to escape for a refreshing breather from the mundane activities of life, but soon my running became the place where I could most easily commune with God. The workout mattered less than the environment it facilitated for a relationship with Him that was free of civilization's distractions. I often found myself praying as I ran. It was a time of solitude and contemplation. It didn't take long for me to discover I needed the chat with Him more than I needed the run.

When I was disappointed after not making the final cut for a SEAL billet at Annapolis, I sat on a solitary boulder in the midst of pine trees in the Rocky Mountains, got out my waterproof notebook, and made a list of everything for which I'm thankful. And now, in my incarceration, I'm discovering that when I focus on His blessings in the past, I am reminded of His character. I know that I can trust Him, even when things don't work out in the present the way I hoped and prayed they would.

Jason continues to do long runs along the perimeter of the prison yard, often covering five to seven miles a day. He chooses the purposeful action of exercise, and it often moves him past the emotional pain of his current circumstances and into personal communication with God through prayer. He keeps his eyes and ears open about who Speak Up for Hope can help—whether inmates or their families. He also devours great books, and he is currently helping two inmate friends to make plans for their soon-coming release dates by getting them connected with educational opportunities.

Jason and his dad are always coming up with new projects to work on together. Most recently they've been talking about types of halfway houses they could develop for inmates newly released from prison. Jason was excited when he was able to line up interim housing for one of his friends who will be released next month. I recently asked him if he would miss his friends as they are freed, and he said, "Mom, I'm thrilled for them. No one would wish for someone to stay in a place like this! They are getting out, and they'll be free!" I could see genuine joy for them in Jason's eyes, and I felt extremely proud of my son.

MARY'S CHOICE

We often think of "action steps" as checking off a to-do list. Building something. Fixing something. Being busy. Joseph, Mary's husband, is a man of action when he finds a place for them to stay in Bethlehem or when he initiates their flight into Egypt. Mary and Joseph act in obedience when they have their baby circumcised and presented at the temple and when they go to Jerusalem for Passover.

Yet all along the way, Mary demonstrates another way to be a woman of action: she is faithful. Perhaps the most amazing thing about Mary is this: her purposeful choice to be resolutely faithful in spite of an unplanned pregnancy, a flight into Egypt to prevent harm to her child, her thoughtful "pondering" of her young son's actions in the temple, her gut-wrenching grief at the crucifixion, her joy with news of the resurrection, all the way to her probable participation in the earliest community of believers.

In Acts 1:12–26, we read the story about the ten days after the Ascension. The apostles and others, including Mary, are living in Jerusalem. The Bible records, "They all met together and were constantly united in prayer, along with Mary the mother of Jesus, several other women, and the brothers of Jesus" (Acts. 1:14 NLT). Mary didn't go back to Galilee after Jesus' crucifixion. She lived with John and participated in this earliest community of believers. She was probably present on Pentecost. She wasn't a leader of the new movement, but she was certainly part of it. Being a part of the earliest community of believers was definitely a purposeful action.

Janet was my best friend in high school. Both of us have faced less-than-ideal situations in our adulthood, even though as teenagers we purposed in our hearts to follow Jesus, no matter what the cost. In a recent phone conversation, Janet summed up my perception of Mary. She said, "I think choosing to remain faithful in the face of deeply disappointing and hurtful circumstances is the most important choice we can make." Because choosing faithfulness is an *internal* action step, we sometimes don't recognize how transformational it is. Mary gave us that example. In the face of unthinkable circumstances, she chose to remain faithful.

THE FIRE FILE

When Jason was first arrested, many people e-mailed Bible verses to us. At that time, we were hurting so badly we could hardly read the Scriptures, and we certainly weren't able to apply them to our lives during such an emotional upheaval. But somehow, I knew there would be a time when I would be able to read those verses, so I collected them in a computer file along with everything connected to Jason's case. I called the file "The Fire." The totality of that file represented the personal hell I felt we had entered—only we were still alive, walking through fire but not consumed.

As time allowed us to breathe again, Gene and I chose the purposeful action of reading God's Word, even though we didn't *feel* like it, and slowly, hope began rising in our hearts. Here are some of the many verses that were saved in that file that continue to help us make hope-filled choices, even when our lives feel completely upside down.

- "We've been surrounded and battered by troubles, but we're not demoralized; we're not sure what to do, but we know that God knows what to do; we've been spiritually terrorized, but God hasn't left our side; we've been thrown down, but we haven't broken" (2 Cor. 4:8–9 MSG).

- "Be brave. Be strong. Don't give up. Expect God to get here soon" (Ps. 31:24 MSG).

- "We continue to shout our praise even when we're hemmed in with troubles, because we know how troubles can develop passionate patience in us, and how that patience in turn forges the tempered steel of virtue, keeping us alert for whatever God will do next" (Rom. 5:3–4 MSG).

- "Though I walk in the midst of trouble, you preserve my life; you stretch out your hand against the anger of my foes, with your right hand you save me. The LORD will fulfill his purpose for me; your love, O LORD, endures forever—do not abandon the works of your hands" (Ps. 138:7–8).

- "So do not fear, for I am with you; do not be dismayed, for I am your God. I will strengthen you and help you; I will uphold you with my righteous right hand" (Isa. 41:10).

- "God's angel sets up a circle of protection around us while we pray" (Psalm 34:7 MSG).

I printed out the Scriptures above (and many more) and began to systematically memorize them. My purposeful action of placing God's Word in my broken heart resulted in surprising personal comfort, and I began praying Scripture over my son.

Lucia Bone faced unthinkable circumstances. She could have allowed a devastating event to destroy her life, but instead, she used the rubble of her situation as a springboard for purposeful action.

A VICTIM AND A VICTOR

I'll never forget that beautiful August afternoon or the excitement in our voices. It was on this day, while vacationing on a beach near where my sister lived in Florida, that Sue and I vowed to grow old together. Even though my sister was eight years older than I, we were like twins (but I rarely allowed her to forget that I was younger!).

Miles separated us, but our daily lives were very similar, and there wasn't a day that went by that we didn't talk, IM, or e-mail between Texas and Florida. It just seemed natural that we would plan to spend our later years together and promise to take care of each other. Although it wouldn't be for another ten to fifteen years, my husband, Mike, and I dreamed about retirement and of living close to Sue. My sister and I dreamed of opening a little shop together (we were both already in the embroidery business). When we finally lived near one another, we would work only at what we loved; we'd play golf and enjoy life. It was our promise to each another.

Two weeks after the day of that promise, all the dreams for our future were shattered in an instant. Nothing could have prepared me for the devastating news I received on August 27, 2001.

A woman murdered on a Monday morning in her home in a nice Orlando neighborhood was big news in Florida. My beloved sister had been tied up, raped, and beaten to death. The cause of death was blunt force trauma to the head, but the murder weapon was never found. After killing her, this brutal criminal had set Sue's body and her home on fire. Ironically, it was a FedEx driver, delivering a package from me, who smelled the smoke and called 911. Sue had already been dead for an hour, but the timing of that delivery saved the evidence the police needed. However, they had no suspect or motive.

I fell to my knees and begged God to make this horrible nightmare stop. Sue was talented, beautiful, intelligent, kind, and lovable. Who would want to harm her? WHY? This was my big sister! Why would God allow this to happen?

Few events of the following weeks remain as vivid as sitting at Sue's memorial service in the small Midwestern town where we grew up. I felt as though my heart was literally broken. The pain was deeper than I ever imagined a hurt could be. Inside I was screaming at God, *I can't do this!* The heavens seemed to reply, *You must!* But I was running—right into God's arms, as it turned out. It was as if He wrapped me in His protective embrace, encouraging me to trust Him. He reminded me that He had created all of us with choices—including Sue's killer, including me. Although it seemed inconceivable, I, too, would have to continue to make choices. I *could* go on with life some-how, and I *must.*

At that moment, I made one more promise to Sue. I would find her killer, and I would make a difference in her memory.

My brother, Bob, headed to Florida to begin the gruesome tasks that would consume our lives for many months to come. Mike and I were to fly to Orlando on September 12, 2001, to meet my brother, the detective assigned to her case, insurance agents, and so on. I dreaded everything about that trip: going to my sister's house, the murder scene, talking to police. The very thought made me sick to my stomach. Sue and I looked so much alike, Mike feared for my safety as well.

As nervous as I was about our trip to Florida the following day, I sat numb to my own pain as I watched the planes fly into the World Trade Center on September 11. My husband, an air-traffic controller, was living the horror many of us were watching unfold on TV. Again, I thought, *Why is God allowing all this horror to happen?* Again, I was reminded that He has graced us with choices. All of us.

We didn't actually make it to Florida until a few weeks later, and as I stepped off the airplane that warm October morning, my sadness at realizing that Sue would never again greet me on arrival with her big dimpled smile, warm hug, and a large mug full of coffee was yet another cruel reminder of what we had lost. How was I going to do any of this: talk to detectives, go to Sue's charred house, smell the smoke, see the bedroom she was raped and murdered in?

It seemed every minute of our time in Orlando was scheduled for Mike and me. We were to have lunch with friends of Sue's and then meet the lead detective at her house immediately following. I hated being in Sue's world without her. These were her friends, her clients, but strangers to me. I had met some of them before, but I didn't know them. For all I knew, one of them could have had something to do with her death! I just wanted to get up and run far away to a safe place where there was no pain. A place where promises would be kept.

After lunch, as we stood in the parking lot, saying good-bye and remembering Sue, I received a phone call with a message from the detective who was solving Sue's murder that very moment. He was sure of who killed her, and he knew where the alleged murderer worked. He was going to make an arrest! I dropped to my knees, crying and trembling uncontrollably. I was unable to get the words out of my mouth to tell Mike what was happening. I just kept saying, "Thank You, God!"

The DNA of the man arrested for burglary, arson, and the rape and first-degree murder of Cathy Sue Weaver matched that of a twice-convicted sex offender who served fewer than thirteen years of a thirty-year sentence for his second rape conviction. By morning, the connection had been made that Sue's killer was a subcontractor of a reputable company she had hired six months before to clean her air ducts.

The next two and a half years were filled with the excruciating disappointment of numerous postponed trial dates. The prosecuting attorney was seeking the death penalty, which only added to the endless postponements. Winning a death sentence would also mean numerous appeals—more trials for us to endure. Would there ever be an end to all of this legal rigmarole?

Out of pure frustration and desperation, Mike and I once again headed to Florida to get some answers. When we first arrived for our appointment with the prosecuting attorney, we were completely taken aback by her suggestion that we accept a plea bargain for Sue's killer in return for his confession. She assured us that he would receive multiple life sentences and that he would never be paroled. He would die in prison, a natural death; there would be no trial and no death sentence.

Ultimately, we accepted the deal. It would still be another month before the sentencing, but Jeffrey Hefling is now serving three life sentences plus thirty years for crimes against my sister, as well as multiple sentences for another rape and parole violations.

When Sue's killer was arrested, Kellie Greene, founder of

SOAR (Speaking Out About Rape) was quoted in the *Orlando Sentinel*: "If someone is a registered sex offender-predator, I don't feel they should have a type of job that would put them inside people's homes . . . For a repeat sex offender to be on community supervision and have access to people in this manner is really frightening."

I contacted Kellie by e-mail, and we established a long-distance friendship. I've admired how Kellie, a rape survivor, has dedicated her life to helping other rape victims and changing legislation requiring harsher sentencing for repeat sex offenders. One of the laws that Kellie has since helped put on the books in Florida might have saved Sue's life had it only been passed earlier. Kellie inspired me and helped me sort through the need I felt to do something meaningful in Sue's memory.

I had no idea what that "something" would be, but I assumed it would involve talking to people—and that made me nervous. I was terrified of public speaking. I struggled to converse with a stranger at a party! Shortly after Sue's death, I read about a Speak Up with Confidence seminar being held at our church. I shocked even myself when I didn't hesitate to enroll—alone. Neither Carol Kent nor I knew at the time how frighteningly similar, yet opposite, our lives had been for the past couple of years. It wasn't until I read *When I Lay My Isaac Down* that I realized that the prosecutor in my sister's case was the same woman who was serving as the D.A. in Orlando when Carol's son went to trial!

I struggled for a couple of years to figure out just what I should do in my sister's memory, but once I got the courage to start my own nonprofit organization, my mission materialized quickly. The Sue Weaver CAUSE (Consumer Awareness of

Unsafe Service Employment) was established in 2004, and our purpose is twofold: to increase public awareness and to advocate for effective safety legislation at local, state, and federal levels. Supported solely by volunteers and donations, we educate consumers and employers regarding the necessity of criminal background checks on all service employees, contractors, and subcontractors hired to work in people's homes.

I now speak in public regularly, sharing my sister's story and advocating for the enactment of laws that can prevent what happened to her from happening to anyone else. I know it's the job I was given to do after losing my big sister. If Sue were alive, she would be keeping an eye on me. I suspect she is doing the same from heaven.[4]

REDEMPTION'S PROMISE

Eugene Peterson writes about the *practice* of resurrection. He calls it "living appropriately and responsively in a world in which Christ is risen."[5] Gene and I are learning that living as true believers, even though our "old" life is shattered, has produced unprecedented opportunities.

I recently received a letter from a thirty-six-year-old man who is incarcerated with Jason. He had read *When I Lay My Isaac Down* and wanted to share with us how it had affected him.

> When I started to read your book, I only made it through a few pages and I began to cry, something I almost never do. I was able to feel the unconditional love of a mother and father for their son. I wasn't crying for my loss, for I have never received

such love. I cried because I knew what a priceless gift I had been denied. I was openly hated by my parents from my earliest memories in life. Thank you for showing me that real love exists . . .

As we began writing to Steve (not his real name), we realized anew that while our new normal is entirely different from what we planned, it can be fulfilling, exciting, encouraging, and purposeful. As we throw our energies into speaking up about our journey and as we continue to develop Speak Up for Hope, a healing is taking place within us. We still have bad days, and I expect they will continue for the rest of our lives. But we have more good days than bad days now. Instead of living only for our own enjoyment, we have a purposeful mission—and it keeps our focus on things that will outlast us.

GOD'S POWER IN YOUR
NEW KIND OF NORMAL

Our new normal can best be summarized with this statement from Lamentations:

I'll never forget the trouble, the utter lostness . . . I remember it all . . . the feeling of hitting the bottom. But there's one other thing I remember . . . I keep a grip on hope: God's loyal love couldn't have run out, His merciful love couldn't have dried up. They're created new every morning. How great your faithfulness! I'm sticking with GOD . . . He's all I've got left." (Lam. 3:19–24 MSG)

1. Are you ever tempted to give up on hope, or are you adjusting to your own new normal with joy? Read through the following list and decide which way of coping you usually prefer when you are going through challenging times:

   - I withdraw from people and try to hide my disappointment and sadness.

   - I get together with one or two close friends and have a pity party.

   - I escape into my favorite addictive pattern (food, work, perfectionism, etc.).

   - I verbalize my frustration to God through prayer.

   - Fill in your own blank.

2. What dreams from your past have had to be readjusted due to circumstances in your life that can't be changed? Have you discovered purpose and meaning in your life even though it is not unfolding as you expected? Devotional author Rebecca Barlow Jordan writes, "Purpose is what drags a pain-riddled body, one leg at a time, to answer the call for something greater than himself."[6] Your situation may not involve physical pain, but to some degree we can all identify with this quote. How have you found purpose and meaning in your own new normal?

3. Gene and I discovered that being honest with people about our son's crime, conviction, and sentencing was much easier than hoping people didn't know and living with "an elephant in the room." On a scale of 1 to 10 (with 10 being the highest), how difficult is it for you to talk to other

people about your own disappointments? If you have been open with others about your circumstances, what has been the result?

4. Read the following verses and write down a core truth in each Scripture that moves you in the direction of purposeful action in the middle of your new normal.

- "It's in Christ that we find out who we are and what we are living for. Long before we first heard of Christ . . . he had his eye on us, had designs on us for glorious living, part of the overall purpose he is working out in everything and everyone" (Eph. 1:11 MSG).

- "You, LORD, give perfect peace to those who keep their purpose firm and put their trust in you" (Isa. 26:3 TEV).

- "Being confident of this, that he who began a good work in you will carry it on to completion until the day of Christ Jesus" (Phil. 1:6).

- "So if you're serious about living this new resurrection life with Christ, act like it. Pursue the things over which Christ presides. Don't shuffle along, eyes to the ground, absorbed with the things right in front of you. Look up, and be alert to what is going on around Christ—that's where the action is. See things from his perspective. Your old life is dead. Your new life, which is your real life—even though invisible to spectators—is with Christ in God. He is your life. When Christ (your real life, remember) shows up again on this earth,

you'll show up, too—the real you, the glorious you"
(Col. 3:1–4 MSG).

5. Think about what my friend Janet said on page 201: "I
think choosing to remain faithful in the face of deeply disappointing and hurtful circumstances is the most important
choice we can make." Do you agree or disagree with that
statement? How do you think Mary, the mother of Jesus,
chose the purposeful action of remaining faithful after
watching her own son's crucifixion? In this book, what
have you learned from the example of Mary that will help
you face the unexpected?

6. Think about the differences between life as you expected it
to be and life as it is for you now. How have unexpected
changes led you to action steps you wouldn't have taken
otherwise? Review the story of Lucia Bone and her decision
to move in a positive direction after the murder of her sister. What prompted her to take action instead of throwing
a permanent pity party after such a devastating loss?
Prayerfully write a list of the new action steps you plan to
take as you purposefully live out the power of Christ's resurrection and the promise of redemption.

Epilogue
COURAGE FOR THE LONG HAUL

*S*ummer returned, marking our first full year in Florida. The hurricane season was much milder than the previous year, and I found myself outside frequently. In our rush to find a house quickly, we had primarily evaluated the inside of the homes we considered and paid little attention to the details of the yard.

But now our move was complete. Walls had been painted, furniture was in place, drapes were hung, my office was functional, and we had discovered which electrical switches were connected to specific lights. We were settled in our home, and the frenzy of activity following our move across the country had surrendered to more normal routines.

I had given up my glorious view of the St. Clair River and the majestic ships that passed outside my window, and I was convinced nothing could take their place. Until now. As Gene and I began to really look at our backyard, we discovered tall, magnificent lilac-colored African lilies, and, to my surprise, our yard displayed its own vibrant orange, white, and blue birds of paradise. There were sweet-scented gardenias and hibiscus in every imaginable color. Elephant's ear provided a tropical accent, and there were multiple varieties of exquisite ornamental grasses. And palm trees were strategically placed, as if an artist had drawn a picture first, and planted them where they would bring the greatest joy. Sandhill cranes frequently graced our yard with their elegant posture and dramatic stance.

Amid the flowers, the former owner had unknowingly prepared my personal quiet time location—a charming bench, under a gazebo, complete with stately cement columns. It was the perfect place to meet with God. Then we discovered a pond on our property that had been overrun with multiple tropical plants. It had its own waterfall and a narrow wooden bridge—and when the overgrowth of the plants was trimmed back, we discovered at least sixty goldfish and koi. I gradually realized God had indeed given me an extraordinary view—far different from the regal ships and blue waters of the St. Clair River, but just as exquisite. I smiled, realizing the splendor in my backyard was a delightful part of my new normal.

That day I recorded my thoughts and later realized I had written a prayer:

Lord, I really didn't want to move to Florida. This state brings back the saddest memories of my life—Jason's trial and conviction, two and a half years of visits to the jail, and now four and a half years of standing in line to visit my son in three different prisons. I've been coming to correctional institutions so long that last week I had to have my photo ID updated. There was a meaningful contrast between the two photographs. The day my initial ID picture was taken I was entering a prison for the first time. Even in a black-and-white photo, my deep sadness and tearful entrance could not be hidden. It was so pitiful I gave it a name—Mama's Mug Shot. But the new photo, taken more than four years later, reflects a broad smile. I can see that the sparkle is back in my eyes. I don't know when the change in my spirit happened, and it has been agonizingly slow, but it's authentic. I hate to admit, even to You, that some parts of my new normal are better than my old normal. I have genuine compassion for pain in the lives of others. My former professionalism has mellowed, and I now have a quiet, humble confidence that I can only hold my head up from day to day with courage that comes from fire-tested faith. I'm more open and honest with people about our journey, and that creates a bond out of which true friendship develops. I'm following Jason's example of listing things I'm thankful for when I'm tempted to drown myself in sorrow. All of that is good—but the process of getting to this point still feels cruel. At least I can be honest with You about that now, knowing You understand and won't judge me for my lack of trust. I may never figure out answers to the "whys" in this unbelievable bend in the road of our lives, and that's okay. Being able to express my anger, hurt, frustration, and honest questions to You, without fear of retribution, is a good part of my new normal. I still sometimes find myself beating into Your chest with my anguish, but I'm leaning into Your irresistible embrace more quickly than in days gone by. I expect we'll

have this tug of war for the rest of my life,
but I now know You love me—and it's okay.

❧

Having courage for the long haul means embracing God's love in the face of unrelenting difficulty. Courage implies tenacity that allows us to hold on to hope that is resistant to opposition and hardship. It is made of a mettle that, over time, has developed a capacity for meeting strenuous challenges with fortitude and resilience. Courage also demonstrates a quality of temperament that enables us to hold on to a positive attitude that is unbroken by repeated disappointments. It is a stubborn but healthy persistence in the face of impossible odds. That is the face of courage. And it is reflected to me in the face of my son.

Last weekend, Gene and I arrived at the prison to visit J.P. After submitting to the strip search all maximum-security inmates must go through in order to meet their family members, he emerged. We embraced and then found a place to sit in the overcrowded room. I listened in as Gene and J.P. made plans to get a large order of greeting cards delivered to the chapel. He said, "The inmates are really low on birthday cards for their families. I did an inventory of what's left last week. Do you think Speak Up for Hope could take on this project?" He smiled and added, "And we're hoping you'll include at least eight thousand Christmas cards in that order, too, so every inmate here at Hardee will have at least five Christmas cards to send to their families and friends during the holidays. Can you work on that, Dad?" Gene agreed to help figure out the details.

I gazed at my son's face, the way mothers do, looking for

small signals that let you know how your child is *really* doing. My mind wandered: *Jason's birthday is coming up next month. He'll be thirty-two years old.* I noticed the beginning signs of graying hair at his temples. *He's graying just the way I did in my early thirties.* An old fear surfaced. *What if he grows old in this prison yard out here in the middle of nowhere? Will anyone still be here to care about him?*

Abruptly, I realized the enemy was trying to steal my joy and dump a truckload of hopelessness in my heart. But he was too late. J.P. was already enthusiastically telling us about the latest book he read and about the class one of our friends is customizing for him. Cathy teaches an entrepreneurship course at a university in Michigan, and she knows J.P. is keenly interested in developing a business plan for his latest dream: a release program for inmates that will provide interim housing, job training, mentorship, and accountability. She had already sent him the textbooks, and he had completed some of the assignments. His passion for this project is intense, and he succeeded in igniting the vision in me.

J.P. leaned forward and said, "I don't want to reinvent the wheel if another nonprofit organization is already doing a good job at this, so let's brainstorm about other ideas too." As our animated conversation continued over the next couple of hours, I realized all three of us were experiencing great joy. Not the kind of happiness that comes when everything turns out the way you hoped, but an enduring joy that comes from knowing you are deeply loved by God. I could almost hear Him whisper, "See, I am doing a new thing! Now it springs up; do you not perceive it? I am making a way in the desert and streams in the wasteland" (Isa. 43:19).

❧

Embracing your new kind of normal is the most empowering choice you will ever make. It transcends common sense. It is resistant to old patterns. It is sticky, uncomfortable, agitating, and difficult. But it is liberating and life giving and spirit enriching. It changes your life and the lives of everyone who joins you on your journey. And then, quite unexpectedly, you realize you are splashing hope into the lives of others because you have an intimate love relationship with the Source of hope.

Living in a new kind of normal has taught me that pain is pain is pain is pain. Repeatedly people come up to Gene and me after speaking engagements, and with urgency they say, "I feel so guilty for feeling sorry for myself. Compared to the suffering you are experiencing, my pain is nothing."

Oh, no—your pain is *very* real. The last seven years have taught us that our pain is no more challenging than the bittersweet struggle my friend Jill experiences with an autistic daughter. Is our pain worse than the mother whose eighteen-year-old son was just killed in Iraq? Is it worse than the pain of a woman who has suffered betrayal at the hands of a spouse who promised to love her forever but left her with young children and a mountain of bills? Is it more intense than the man injured in an accident who is now paralyzed? No—pain is pain. It's *all* pain.

So how do we find courage for the long haul? How does Jason Kent keep holding on to hope in the face of an endless sentence? How do we, his parents, not only make it through the next day, but begin to make choices that result in triumphant living, without minimizing the intensity of our sorrow? There's only one way: by experiencing the unconditional love of God that we in turn splash all over the people around us. Experiencing His irresistible love in the middle of catastrophic loss (or even during life's inevitable challenges and disappointments) is so empowering that we automatically keep passing it on to other people. And we live in the constant astonishment that God uses broken people to minister to broken people.

Mary's life demonstrated that principle. She had watched her son suffer and followed him all the way to the foot of the cross. Yet somehow she managed to believe and internalize the words of Gabriel and Elizabeth in Luke 1: "You are highly favored. The Lord is with you. Blessed are you among women" (see verses 28 and 42). When we are "blessed," we are on the right road going in the right direction. We sense that we have been "favored" with a surprising joy that surpasses suffering. We can hear the Father's voice saying, "I have loved you with an everlasting love; I have drawn you with loving-kindness" (Jer. 31:3). When we internalize the truth that He loves us, that conviction about our identity is foundational to our resilience in suffering.

As we embrace God's unconditional love, Gene and I sense that we have been granted a *privilege* (as unwanted as it might be) to hold up His name to the world around us in the face of hopeless circumstances. There is a trust in our hearts that Jason's life will be powerfully used of God—whether he is *never* released from prison, or if by some miracle, he eventually walks in freedom. His life will be valuable, purposeful, and significantly used by the Father who loves him.

Amy Carmichael wrote, "I think it must hurt the tender love of our Father when we press for reasons for His dealings with us, as though He were not Love, as though not He, but another chose our inheritance for us, and as though what He chose to allow could be less than the very best and dearest that Love Eternal had to give."[1]

I want to insist that my prayers get answered with the favorable resolution I have requested. But God says, *Carol, I have a bigger plan than you envisioned for this situation. You think your life has fallen apart, but I have a salvage operation in motion that will reach way beyond your family. Trust Me. And while you wait, you will experience that I am very close to the brokenhearted. I will not leave you or walk away from You. Keep holding on to hope.*

ABOUT THE AUTHOR

$\mathcal{C}$arol Kent is a best-selling author and a gifted public speaker who is known for being dynamic, humorous, encouraging, and biblical. Carol has spoken internationally and regularly appears on a wide variety of nationally syndicated radio and television broadcasts. She is the president of a Christian speakers' bureau and the founder and director of Speak Up with Confidence seminars. She has also founded the nonprofit organization Speak Up for Hope, which benefits the families of incarcerated individuals. More information is available at www.CarolKent.org.

ACKNOWLEDGMENTS

$\mathscr{A}$ book this personal could not have been written without the loving support of my husband, Gene Kent. He opened his journals, his raw emotions, and his spiritual journey (and the not-so-spiritual parts) of the past seven years and gave me permission to write honestly about our ongoing experience.

My respect for the brave women who told their personal stories in this book is off the charts. Louise Tucker Jones, Karan Gleddie, Lynn D. Morrissey, Sandra Aldrich, Lisa Ramsland, Sandra Troutman, and Lucia Bone exposed their deepest hurts in order to reveal God's miraculous healing power. I am also thankful to the contributors who cannot be named because of the personal nature of their stories. Your bravery and courage provide an example of what it means to hold on to hope when life turns upside down.

This story could not have been written without the ongoing support of family members and friends who have continued to engage in this never-ending marathon. Special thanks go out to Kathy Blume and our ministry intercessors, Pastor Kim Moore, Kathe Wunnenberg, Jan Fleck, Cathy Gallagher, Dr. Don and Anne Denmark, Ginger Shaw, Kay Jelinek, Maureen O'Neill, and to our Stretcher Bearers.

As the nonprofit organization Speak Up for Hope continues to grow, we are grateful for the tireless efforts of my mother, Pauline Afman, my sister Bonnie Afman Emmorey, and Penny Williams, LLP. A shout-out also goes to the corrections officers and prison chaplains who treat the inmates with decency and respect.

Traci Mullins of Eclipse Editorial Services provided guidance, extraordinary editorial expertise, and the gentle compassion of a friend as this book was shaped into a final manuscript. Karen Lee-Thorp and my sister Jennie Afman Dimkoff offered valuable biblical insights. Our remarkable administrative assistant, Shirley Liechty, kept our office running smoothly during the completion of this project.

Finally, I am grateful for my new relationship with Thomas Nelson, Inc. David Moberg first caught the vision for this project, and Carolyn Denny provided valuable feedback as she championed this manuscript.

NOTES

PROLOGUE

1. Taken from *Grace Disguised* by Gerald L. Sittser. Copyright © 2004.Used by permission of Zondervan.
2. Copyright 1985 Cook Communications Ministries. *You Gotta Keep Dancin'* by Tim Hansel. May not be further reproduced. All rights reserved.

CHAPTER 1

1. Charles Colson, as quoted by Lloyd Cory, *Quotable Quotations* (Wheaton, IL: Victor Books, 1985), 214.
2. Louise Tucker Jones can be contacted at LouiseTJ@cox.net or at www.LouiseTuckerJones.com for speaking and personal inquiries.
3. Ken Gire, *The North Face of God* (Wheaton, IL: Tyndale House Publishers, Inc., 2005), 120. Used by permission. All rights reserved.

CHAPTER 2

1. Brennan Manning, *Ruthless Trust* (San Francisco: HarperCollins, 2000), 178.
2. Syeda Ferguson, *Times Herald*, Port Huron, MI, November 24, 1999, 3A.
3. Visit Karan K. Gleddie's web site at www.karangleddie.com, or contact her at karan@karangleddie.com.
4. Merriam-Webster, Inc. *Merriam-Webster's collegiate dictionary*, 10th ed. (Springfield, Mass.: Merriam-Webster, 1996).
5. Sandra Aldrich is president of Bold Words, Inc. and can be contacted at boldwords@aol.com for speaking and personal inquiries.
6. Nancy Guthrie, *Holding on to Hope* (Wheaton, IL: Tyndale, 2002), 58.
7. Brennan Manning, 178.

CHAPTER 3

1. Ken Gire, *The North Face of God* (Wheaton, IL: Tyndale House Publishers, Inc., 2005), 120. Used by permission. All rights reserved.
2. This historical information on taxation is based on F.C. Grant, *The Economic Background of the Gospels*, (Oxford, 1926), p. 105; cited in F.F. Bruce, *New Testament History*, (New York: Doubleday, 1969), 40.
3. Jan Frank, *A Graceful Waiting* (Ventura, CA: Servant Publications, a division of Regal Books, 1996), 188. Used by permission of Regal Books, Ventura, CA 93003.
4. Ben Patterson, *Waiting: Finding Hope When God Seems Silent* (Downer's Grove,

IL: InterVarsity Press, 1989), 111.

5. Jan Frank, 188.

CHAPTER 4

1. Taken from *Grace Disguised* by Gerald L. Sittser. Copyright © 2004. Used by permission of Zondervan.

2. Adapted from *The Life Application Bible, NIV* (Wheaton, IL: Tyndale House Publishers, Inc. and Grand Rapids, MI: Zondervan Publishing House, Notes and Helps, 1991), 1992.

3. Fanny Crosby, "To God Be the Glory," © 1875.

4. Rebecca Barlow Jordan, *40 Days in God's Blessing*, (New York: Warner Faith, 2006), 106.

CHAPTER 5

1. Brenda Waggoner, *The Velveteen Woman* (Colorado Springs: Chariot Victor, a division of Cook Communications, 1999), 162. All rights reserved. Brenda Waggoner can be contacted through www.brendawaggoner.com.

2. Merriam-Webster, Inc. *Merriam-Webster's collegiate dictionary*, 10th ed. (Springfield, Mass.: Merriam-Webster, 1996).

3. Jennie Afman Dimkoff, *Unexpected Grace*, (Grand Rapids, MI: Revell, a division of Baker Publishing Group, 2005), 137.

4. Ralph Gower, *The New Manners and Customs of Bible Times* (Chicago: Moody Press, 1987), 65.

5. Max Lucado, *A Life Worth Giving* (Nashville: W Publishing Group, a division of Thomas Nelson, Inc., 2002). Reprinted by permission. All rights reserved.

6. Excerpted from *Love Letters to God* © 2004 by Lynn D. Morrissey. Used by permission of Multnomah Publishers, a division of Random House, Inc.

7. Excerpted from *Your God is Too Safe* © 2001 by Mark Buchanan. Used by permission of Multnomah Publishers, a division of Random House, Inc.

8. Brenda Waggoner, 162.

CHAPTER 6

1. Jack Hayford, *The Mary Miracle* (Ventura, CA: Regal Books, 1994), 158. Used by permission of Regal Books, Ventura, CA 93003.

2. The term "Stretcher Bearers" refers to the passage in Luke 5:17-30 where people hear that Jesus is in town. Some men carry their friend, a paralyzed man, on a stretcher to the home where Jesus is healing people. However, the crowd is so large, they weren't able to get close to Jesus—so they got

creative. They climbed up on the roof, made a hole in the roof, and dropped their friend down to Jesus. The Bible says Jesus healed the man and forgave his sins. People were awestruck, because they had never seen anything like this before. When our own Stretcher Bearers began meeting our needs for prayer and for tangible help, we, too, were awestruck with how much support we had in the middle of our deepest sorrow.

3. J.I. Packer, quoted in *A Window on Hope* (Lombard, IL: Christian Art Gifts, 2003), 16.

4. Excerpted from *As Silver Refined* © 1997 by Kay Arthur. Used by permission of WaterBrook Press, a division of Random House, Inc.

5. Lisa Ramsland can be contacted through www.lisaramsland.com for speaking or other inquiries.

6. Jack Hayford, 158.

7. Merriam-Webster, Inc. *Merriam-Webster's collegiate dictionary*, 10th ed. (Springfield, Mass.: Merriam-Webster, 1996).

8. Kay Arthur, 255.

CHAPTER 7

1. Elisa Morgan, quoted in *Closer to God*, (Wheaton, IL: Tyndale, 1996), 134.

CHAPTER 8

1. Jan Johnson, *Living a Purpose-Full Life*, (Colorado Springs: Waterbrook Press, 1999), 200.

2. For additional information, go to www.SpeakUpWithConfidence.com.

3. Jan Johnson, 2001.

4. For more information, go to www.SpeakUpforHope.org.

5. To learn more about CAUSE, visit the website at www.sueweavercause.org, or contact Lucia Bone at lucia@sueweavercause.org or 214-450-5812.

6. Eugene Peterson, *Living the Resurrection*, (Colorado Springs: NavPress, 2006), 14.

7. Rebecca Barlow Jordan, *40 Days in God's Blessing*, New York, Boston, Nashville: Warner Faith, 2006), 62.

EPILOGUE

1. Amy Carmichael, *Rose from Brier* (Fort Wayne, PA: Christian Literature Crusade, 1972).

*S*PEAK UP FOR HOPE

is a nonprofit organization that seeks to
live out the principle of Proverbs 31:8-9 (MSG):

"Speak up for the people who have no voice,
for the rights of all the down-and-outers.
Speak out for justice.
Stand up for the poor and destitute!"

To accomplish this mission, we will:

- Assist churches in working with prisons to provide hands-on encouragement to inmates and their families by adopting one prison family, and developing a network of resources to assist that family spiritually, financially, and personally.

- Network educators with prison wardens and chaplains in order to provide GED programs, marriage and family classes, vocational training, and college credit programs that will give purpose to prisoners and help to ensure personal success after an inmate is released.

- Connect families of prisoners with Christian counselors at reduced fees.

- Provide mentoring for spouses and children of inmates.

- Network business professionals with soon-to-be-released inmates to offer job opportunities that provide a chance for a fresh start.

- Assist women's ministry groups with launching the "Boxes of Encouragement"project that provides gifts to wives and mothers of inmates.

It is the goal of Speak Up for Hope to give hope to the hopeless, encouragement and strength to the weary, reparation to marriages that have been torn apart by incarceration, and mental, spiritual, and physical stability to the children of prisoners.

We pray that people all over the world will begin speaking up for those who cannot speak up for themselves. As people become the hands and feet of Jesus to "the least of these," something miraculous happens. As we choose to get personally involved by giving, volunteering, and praying, we are transformed from the inside out as we model for others how to become hope givers.

Carol Kent

Carol Kent, Founder

Gene Kent

Gene Kent, Director

For more information on the variety of ways in which you can be involved in Speak Up for Hope, please contact:

SPEAK UP FOR HOPE
P.O. Box 6262
Lakeland, FL 33807-6262
www.SpeakUpforHope.org
888.987.1212

Make tax-deductible contributions payable to Speak Up for Hope or donations can be made online at www.SpeakUpforHope.org.